The Philanthropic Executive

Establishing a Charitable Plan for Individuals and Businesses

By Howard M. Weiss

Published by Aspatore, Inc.

For corrections, company/title updates, comments or any other inquiries please email info@aspatore.com.

First Printing, 2003
10 9 8 7 6 5 4 3 2 1

www.Aspatore.com

Aspatore Books is the largest and most exclusive publisher of C-Level executives (CEO, CFO, CTO, CMO, Partner) from the world's most respected companies. Aspatore annually publishes C-Level executives from over half the Global 500, top 250 professional services firms, law firms (MPs/Chairs), and other leading companies of all sizes. By focusing on publishing only C-Level executives, Aspatore provides professionals of all levels with proven business intelligence from industry insiders, rather than relying on the knowledge of unknown authors and analysts. Aspatore Books is committed to publishing a highly innovative line of business books, redefining and expanding the meaning of such books as indispensable resources for professionals of all levels. In addition to individual best-selling business titles, Aspatore Books publishes the following unique lines of business books: Inside the Minds, Business Bibles, Bigwig Briefs, C-Level Business Review (Quarterly), Book Binders, ExecRecs, and The C-Level Test, innovative resources for all professionals. Aspatore is a privately held company headquartered in Boston, Massachusetts, with employees around the world.

The Philanthropic Executive

Table of Contents

ONE

FROM SHAREHOLDER TO COMMUNITY VALUE

Enron, Worldcom, Adelphia – sinister household names now associated with the heights of corporate greed, corruption, and malfeasance. Their CEOs and CFOs are facing disgrace and even handcuffs. One of the world's most advanced accounting firms, Arthur Andersen, now lies in ruin, as Enron was one of its clients. What appear to have been the crimes of a sinister few also blocked the recovery of a struggling stock market. Acting more aggressively than usual, lawmakers and the President forged legislation to raise penalties for corporate malfeasance and required CEOs to affirm the integrity of their companies', financial statements on August 14, 2002.

While this crisis is particularly disturbing because it hit the integrity of the financial and accounting systems, corporate CEOs have faced troubles before. The robber barons of the late 18th century amassed great fortunes while knocking out competitors and treating workers harshly, only to be confronted later by Teddy Roosevelt and anti-trust legislation, along with the rise of labor unions. In more modern times, corporate raiders (such as T. Boone Pickens) launched takeover bids of some of the nation's leading companies, cutting staff and closing facilities to gain greater operating efficiencies. Some communities suffered with the loss of business and jobs and pinned the blame on corporate leadership – either the CEO of the acquiring company or even the CEO of the target company – for not maintaining shareholder value at a high enough level.

Throughout history, those trials and tribulations of the CEO resulted from an evolutionary process as the captains of industry always tried to adapt to the challenges of their competitive business environment. First were the industrialists. During the late 19th century, mass production techniques greatly expanded the production capacity of American industry, far outstripping the consuming power of the nation. Consequently, the economy went through periods of intense price competition as corporations witnessed vanishing profits. As a result, business combinations and mergers formed, and near monopolies emerged in several important industries, including oil, sugar, tobacco, steel, and farm machinery. Leaders of these powerful companies became known as "robber barons" because they drove out many of their smaller competitors and thus dominated the U.S. economy.

Let's next look at the corporate raiders who emerged during the 1980s. Years of languishing stock prices, from 1966 until 1982, left many companies worth far more than their stock market capitalization indicated. Some companies had valuable assets, such as oil and natural resources or a strong customer franchise. In others, company management had not harnessed the true earnings power of the firm. Accordingly, great "values" existed in the market, and it was cheaper for one company to buy another than to develop new products or enter new markets from scratch. Still other industries, such as banking, had far too many firms competing, and there were great savings to be realized through mergers. These business activities gave rise to the feared corporate raiders, such as T. Boone Pickens, but also led to the famed insider trading scandals that featured such notables as Ivan Boskey and Michael Milken.

This brings us to the present CEO scandals. Learning from their compatriots of the 1980s, whose companies were acquired and who were then given a ticket to early retirement, today's CEOs and their boards realized that their key to survival lay in creating ever increasing shareholder value. Boards fired chief executives who did not deliver profits and higher stock prices. At the same time, and more than ever before, they aligned executive compensation with the firm's stock price. Accordingly, the fortunes of a company's executives became directly tied to the same fortunes of its shareholders, as these executives now became substantial shareholders themselves. Their compensation has centered on stock ownership in the form of options, grants, or long-term deferred compensation plans.

The intense focus on shareholder value, while inherently a sound concept, enabled a different type of CEO to evolve. Wall Street punished companies that missed quarterly earnings targets, CEOs became intensely focused on hitting those targets. Accordingly, some CEOs and their top executives were encouraged to make decisions that enhanced their ability to reach those quarterly numbers even if it meant pushing accounting rules to the limit. While most executives certainly played by the rules, a few did not. The extreme cases involved misappropriating expenses and establishing fraudulent off-balance sheet entities to prop up financial balance sheets and earnings.

As is the case with any dramatic news event, the media coverage was intense in reporting the latest financial scandals. Two very different cover stories from competing business magazines were perhaps the most impactful in portraying the modern CEO. In its November 18, 2002, issue, *Fortune* launched a cover story titled "The CEO Under Fire: Inside the world of today's embattled chief executive." Through a series of articles, *Fortune* writers provided insight into how the current crises evolved and how enormous compensation packages contributed to the corruption of some executives. Just two weeks later, *Business Week* launched a cover story focused on CEOs but from a vastly different angle. In a special report titled "The New Face of Philanthropy," *Business Week* speaks of the tremendous transformation taking place in the field of philanthropy. This change is not led by religious or political leaders, but by the country's super-rich corporate executives and entrepreneurs.

The timing of these two leading cover stories may be coincidental; nevertheless, there is a definite link between them. Among the underlying messages is that personal philanthropy is not only good for a business but is also good for the image of its CEO. Additionally, innovative charitable endeavors can take some of the sting out of the lavish compensation many executives receive, particularly as some of those funds get channeled to charitable works.

The changes going on in today's philanthropic world are the most widespread since the days of Carnegie and Rockefeller. While amassing their wealth, these individuals earned the disdain of many. Today, however, people associate the Carnegie name more with libraries, museums, and music halls than they do with steel. Likewise, the Rockefeller name today is associated more often with the world's pre-eminent foundation than the pre-eminent power of oil. Both of these men created the modern world of philanthropy, pursuing the transformation of their own "shareholder" wealth into "community" wealth. Carnegie best expressed his thoughts on this issue in 1899 in his writing, "The Gospel of Wealth":

Rich men should be thankful for one inestimable boom. They have it in their power during their lives to busy themselves in organizing benefactions from which the masses of their fellows will derive lasting advantage, and thus dignify their own lives.

A hundred years later, Bill Gates, Ted Turner, and George Soros are leading a modern cadre of executive philanthropists to usher in a new era of charitable giving. They and their contemporaries are both putting up big dollars and offering their entrepreneurial and organizational skills to the causes they seek to support. They are taking the skills that enabled them to create enormous shareholder value to communities around the country and the world. Essentially, they are striving to achieve a level of success in altering the social landscape that is comparable to their success in the commercial arena. Even Michael Milken, whom we were critical of earlier for his role in the insider trading activities of the 1980's, emerged as one of the nation's leading philanthropists. The Milken Family Foundation, now in its 22nd year, is a significant supporter of education initiatives and a broad range of medical research.

Benefits of Philanthropic Leadership

The essential purpose of this book is twofold. First, we want to issue a clarion call to executives to formulate their own personal – not just corporate – philanthropic plans. Second, we want to provide the executive with a holistic process to formulate those plans. Before doing this, let's look at why an executive would want to have an extensive philanthropic game plan that goes beyond just writing checks in the spirit of being a good corporate and community citizen.

Financial

The bottom line for the executive is that you can realize important financial benefits with certain charitable structures. As we will show later, you can realize current income tax deductions with charitable gifts. Additionally, you can escape the onerous estate and gift taxes by contributing assets to charitable structures. Equally important, specific charitable structures provide a way to effectively diversify away from a low-cost-basis concentrated stock position and provide the donor with not only tax advantages, but also a degree of cash flow. This can serve executives well as they move to lessen the overall exposure to their company stock.

Directing Children

One of the greater challenges facing corporate executives and other wealthy individuals is how to raise children under great affluence. Some families turn to philanthropy and family foundations as one vehicle to facilitate social and community responsibility. Directing children to accomplish charitable deeds with high impact can lead to useful lives and a greater sense of overall responsibility.

Making an Impact

In its December 2, 2002, cover story on philanthropy, *Business Week* displayed two lists. One list contained the names of the 50 most generous philanthropists; the other, the most innovative philanthropists. As you peruse the lists, you notice that these individuals, predominately corporate executives and entrepreneurs, seem to get involved in activities where they believe they can make a deciding impact. They seek to transform something or to aggressively deal with a particular social or human problem in a focused way.

Accordingly, you can get involved to affect a community, an institution, or a policy. For example, within a community you can help re-build a depressed inner-city neighborhood through job training, building affordable housing, or helping residents start a business. Alternatively, you might want to make a significant impact on a local institution, such as a school, art museum, symphony, zoo, or hospital. On a larger scale, your interest could lie in such organizations as the American Heart Association or Amnesty International. Finally, you and your family may become deeply engaged in pursuing policy changes, such as medical care reform, in your community or beyond.

Extending Your Entrepreneurial Zeal

The social sector offers the entrepreneurial executive a boundless opportunity to apply practices that were successful in their own business to the non-profit world. Technological advances, innovative financing, and creative marketing techniques can be transformed from the business world to attack the problems inherent in education, poverty, and healthcare. Moreover, the intense analytical processes used to build and maintain successful companies can be applied to benchmarking the results that need to be achieved in the social sector.

Take, for example, Eli Broad, the founder of Sun America and Kaufman & Broad. He is attempting to transfer his entrepreneurial skills to deal with problems in education. Using novel approaches, Broad develops programs to better train school leadership in all facets of managing the education process. He even offers rewards for successful performance among the schools.

Leaving a Legacy

Finally, philanthropy enables you to leave a lasting legacy, which can take different forms. You can leave your legacy with an institution, such as a hospital where you may want to build a cancer center. Alternatively, your legacy can be with a scholarship fund where your endowment continuously gives students the opportunity to gain an education. Finally, you may want your family name to live in perpetuity through a private family foundation.

Creating a Charitable Plan

Once you decide to embark on a philanthropic path, you will need to develop an appropriate plan. There are three legs to the stool of a successful philanthropic plan, and we will cover each extensively in the succeeding chapters:

Structure

You can choose among several charitable structures, each offering distinct features in tax and estate planning benefits, grant-making flexibility, costs, time horizon, and investment management options. One size does not fit all, so it is important to put in place the right structure. It also may be appropriate to use more than one structure within an integrated plan.

Investments

Each structure presents its own investment options. In today's turbulent world of investments, managing the charitable portfolio effectively is paramount to achieving your overall philanthropic goals. This is no longer a passive activity, so a strong game plan needs to be developed and implemented.

Grant-making

After your structure or structures are in place and your investment plan developed, you are then positioned to develop programs for distributing the assets. A complete program not only deals with who gets the money but also covers processes for evaluating grants, benchmarking grantee performance and methods for releasing the funds (multi-year and gift-matching, for example).

Navigating with This Guide

We are now ready to embark on creating your philanthropic plan. The book covers all three legs of the stool in the following format.

We begin by considering the range of structural options along with the advantages and disadvantages of each. Chapter 2 covers the traditional structures of lifetime gifts, while Chapter 3 goes into depth on the features and benefits of charitable trusts. We cover the world of foundations in Chapter 4, which also encompasses community foundations and supporting organizations. We then devote Chapter 5 to a brief synopsis of some advanced techniques, along with creative ways to employ them.

Once you have your structure in place, you have to fund it with certain assets. In Chapter 6 we cover the assets you can or cannot contribute to the various charitable structures, as well as the tax implications surrounding each. After covering each of these structures, we then devote Chapter 7 to the issue of diversifying away from a concentrated stock holding, particularly a low-cost-basis one. We will demonstrate how certain charitable vehicles can fit into an overall plan to manage a large equity position. This chapter actually ties the plan together.

Moving on, we will deal comprehensively with the investment of fund assets in Chapter 8, demonstrating how you establish a comprehensive investment policy for a foundation. Grant-making is covered in Chapters 9 and 10. Chapter 9 explains how to establish a complete grant-making plan, and Chapter 10 highlights some of the significant new themes emerging in the field. Chapter 11 outlines the roles of the key professionals and advisers you may need as you proceed. In Chapter 12, we survey the resources available in the marketplace, including print literature, Web sites, and organizations.

Finally, we offer a concluding chapter on leadership. While this book appears to be heavily focused on the corporate executive with significant company stock holdings, the contents truly apply to anyone who wants to establish a philanthropic plan. Also, while we frequently discuss using single stock holdings to contribute to charitable vehicles, there are many other types of assets you can elect to contribute.

TWO

TRADITIONAL STRUCTURES – LIFETIME GIFTS

Upon making that key decision to embark on a philanthropic plan beyond just writing checks at year-end, you face the daunting task of deciding where to begin. One might argue that the proper starting point on the journey is to decide which charities or which field of interest you wish to pursue and then build everything around that. Others will suggest that you keep your grant-making flexible and first decide which vehicles or legal structures offer you not only the grant-making flexibility you want but also the most effective tax and estate-planning benefits. I will not offer a hard and fast rule, but for the sake of presenting a plan in an orderly fashion, we will begin with structure. It is important to note, however, that the philanthropic plan needs to be integrated across structure, investments, and grant-making with appropriate adjustments made along the way.

As we evaluate the different legal structures, we'll look first at the more traditional ones. Then we will examine some variations of these traditional structures, along with other advanced techniques.

Among the traditional structures or techniques are the following:

- Outright Gifts
- Life Income Gifts
  - Charitable gift annuities
  - Deferred gift annuities
  - Pooled income funds

- Charitable Trusts
  - Charitable remainder annuity trust
  - Charitable remainder unitrust
  - Charitable lead annuity trust
  - Charitable lead unitrust
- Foundation Structures
  - Community foundations
  - Donor-advised funds
  - Supporting organizations
  - Private foundations

We will consider each of these structures in turn, demonstrating how it works, its advantages and disadvantages, and when it is applicable.

Before describing these various techniques, it is important to note that each involves a series of tax and legal considerations. For example, in each case there are income, gift, and estate tax issues. Furthermore, the current tax laws are somewhat in flux with the passage of The Economic Growth and Tax Relief Reconciliation Act of 2001 (TEGTRRA). Estate tax rates are scheduled to decline through 2009 and then be eliminated for one year only, unless Congress enacts a permanent repeal. However, with increasing budget deficits and a host of other factors that could arise, it will be difficult to project future tax polices.

Accordingly, while this book contains a number of illustrated legal structures, it is by no means intended to be a formal legal or tax guide and should not be relied on as such. Furthermore, it is not intended to be complete in all aspects. Instead, its purpose is only to prompt discussion and thought by demonstrating the applicability of various structures for the corporate executive, business owner, or other wealthy individual who wishes to establish philanthropic programs. It is therefore important to consult your attorney, CPA, or financial adviser before establishing a specific program, as there are many fine points to consider.

OUTRIGHT GIFTS

Perhaps the simplest of all charitable structures is the outright gift of cash, securities, or other property. These gifts provide an immediate estate, gift, and income tax deduction of some kind. The issues surrounding outright gifts include the following:

- Income tax deductions are limited to a percentage of your adjustable gross income (AGI).

- The limitation depends on the type of charity that receives the gift and the type of property donated.

- Income tax deductions are also influenced by the appreciation built into each asset. Some assets will give you the ability to deduct fair market value, while others will provide you with only the cost basis.

- Tax deductions are also influenced by whether or not the charity has the immediate use of the funds.

In subsequent sections we will cover these limitations as they apply to structures and contributed property.

LIFE INCOME GIFTS

Life income gifts are essentially split-interest gifts that provide benefits to both you and the charity. To you, the donor, these gifts can provide an income stream coupled with income and estate tax benefits. To the charity flows a future irrevocable gift. We will cover the three most common life income gifts. In deciding which is more appropriate, the important factors will include your age, type of asset to be contributed, and timing of cash flows.

Charitable Gift Annuities

One of the more popular forms of giving to a preferred charity, the charitable gift annuity is essentially a contract between you and a qualified charity. You transfer cash or securities to the charity in return for a promise to pay an annuity for your lifetime. It is also possible to have the annuity last for the lifetime of both you and your spouse. Upon the death of the annuitants, the charity receives the remaining funds. For the remainder gift to charity, you receive an immediate income tax deduction. Acceptable assets to fund these structures include cash, securities, and real estate that can easily be sold. Universities, hospitals, and religious institutions represent the most prevalent issuers of gift annuities.

How It Works

Here is how you would structure a charitable gift annuity. After selecting your charity and determining the amount you wish to transfer, the following steps generally take place:

1. Determine how much your annuity will be and how frequently (monthly, quarterly, or annually) you will be paid. Your payout is not unlimited. Money must be left for the charity after the annuity payments. Additionally, the philanthropic world would not be well served if charities aggressively competed for funds on the basis of payout percentages alone. Therefore, an organization called the American Council on Gift Annuities recommends rates that charities apply to annuitants. It publishes tables for both single-life and two-life gift contracts. The tables are established so that approximately 50 percent of the initial contributions will end up with the charity. The organization you work with will have all of the software tools to calculate these numbers, as well as those that follow.

2. The charity will then need to provide you with a calculation for your charitable gift for purposes of your current income tax deduction. To arrive at this figure, they will first need to calculate the present value of your annuity stream and then subtract it from the initial gift. The present value is determined by applying an annuity factor to your annual payment. The annuity factor is determined by your age, the IRS Section 7520 Rate, and the frequency of payments. The Section 7520 rate is called the Applicable Federal Rate (AFR) and is set monthly by the Internal Revenue Service. This is the rate the IRS assumes an investment will return over a stated time period and is used to value lifetime annuity streams and remainder interests. Applying this rate to the principal balance will determine the growth of the assets over time. From this amount, you can then subtract the value of the annuity stream to arrive at the value of the reminder interest. We will highlight how these numbers interact in the illustration below.

3. The final calculation is used to arrive at a breakdown of the components of each annuity payment. Generally, each annuity payment will consist of three portions:

    *   Return of capital
    *   Ordinary income
    *   Capital gain

Again, the charity will have software to calculate these numbers for you. However, there are some important tax concepts to consider when establishing these structures:

1. Part of your annuity payment will be a return of your initial funds. The cash portion and cost basis of securities transferred will flow back to you on a tax-free basis.

2. If you contribute appreciated securities, such as your company stock, a part of your annuity will represent capital gains and will be taxed at the capital gains rate. This is not as bad as it sounds, since you are able to spread out the gain on your initial contribution over the life of the annuity.

3. The third part of the Annuity represents current earnings on the principal. As we mentioned earlier, the fund is expected to grow at the Applicable Federal Rate.

4. This three-part income tax treatment generally lasts until you reach your life expectancy. At that time, it is assumed that you regained your initial investment and exhausted your capital gains on the original property. Accordingly, future annuity payments would be considered as ordinary income.

5. There are gift and estate tax implications as well on charitable gift annuities. If you die before receiving your initial investment, your estate is entitled to an income tax deduction on the remaining amount of principal not yet distributed. The remainder gift at that time would then be offset by a charitable deduction. It is also important to note that if an individual other than you or your spouse is the annuitant, the value of the annuity is considered to be a gift, and you may be subject to gift taxes if it is beyond your annual exclusion at the time.

Illustration

To better understand the conceptual framework, consider the illustration below. We will start off with these assumptions:

1. You are currently *65 years old* and wish to establish a *$100,000 charitable gift annuity* at your college. You are contributing company stock holdings that have a *cost basis of $30,000.*

2. You have arranged with the University to provide you with a *6.8 percent single lifetime annuity* as delineated in the American Council on Gift Annuities rate schedule for an individual 65 years of age. The *annuity will be paid semiannually.*

3. We will assume a federal *AFR of 5 percent.*

We will first calculate the charitable gift:

Annuity payment:

$100,000 x 6.8% = $6,800

Annuity factor (65 years old at AFR of 5%):

10.5490

Annuity adjustment factor (for semiannual payment):

1.0167

Present value of annuity:

$6,800 x 10.5490 x 1.0167 = $72,931

Charitable gift deduction:

$100,000 - 72,931 = $27,069

We then break out the annuity payment into its basis, gain, and ordinary income portions:

Expected Return Multiple (from life expectancy tables):

19

Allocated basis:

$30,000 x (72,931 ÷ 100,000) = $21,879

Allocated gain:

$72,931 - 21,879 = $51,052

Expected return:

$6,800 x (19 x 1.0167) = $131,358

Exclusion ratio:

$72,931 ÷ 131,358 = 55.5%

Exclusion (basis and gain):

$6,800 x 55.5% = $3,774

Ordinary income portion:

$ 6,800 - 3,774 = $3,026

Gain portion:

$51,052 ÷ (19 x 1.0167) = $2,643

Basis portion:

$6,800 - (3,026 + 2,643) = $1,131

It is not so important at this juncture to understand all of the math. We showed it here just to illustrate that there is a mathematical calculation that a charity (for example, your university) will provide to you upon creating a charitable gift annuity.

Let's summarize what you just did:

- You established a charitable gift annuity to benefit your college at $100,000.
- You will receive a lifetime annuity from the gift of $6,800.
- You get an immediate charitable income tax deduction of $27,069 for the remainder interest going to the school.
- Your annual annuity is broken out into an ordinary income portion of $3,026; a capital gain portion of $2,643, and a tax- free return of capital portion of $1,131.

Advantages

1. You receive an immediate charitable income deduction that can generally range from 25 percent to 50 percent, depending on your age and the timing of your annuity payments.
2. The income annuity is generally greater than what you could earn from most money market or even fixed income investments.
3. Part of your annuity represents the tax-free return of your original capital.
4. This is an efficient way to benefit a charity.
5. Although you would not totally escape capital gains tax on a low-basis stock that you contribute, you will be able to defer the gain over an extended time period.

Disadvantages

1. When setting up a charitable gift annuity, you rely on the charity to be around to complete the payment of your annuity. Your gift is irrevocable, and you must rely on the full faith and credit of the charity to realize your payments. However, some charities will purchase insurance to protect their gift annuities.
2. Unlike a charitable remainder trust or foundation, you cannot name several charitable beneficiaries. The gift annuity is issued by a particular charity and can benefit only that charity.
3. You do not have influence over the investment of the funds. But you are tied to the contracted annuity, so it may not matter.

Who uses this vehicle?

1. This is a good technique for the executive who wants to benefit a known charity with a leveraged gift. A common type of charity would be your alma mater or a large religious organization, where

you are likely to maintain your loyalty and would not mind being committed to a specific organization.

2. It can be an efficient way for part of your concentrated, low-basis equity position, particularly if the dividend is low. While achieving a charitable deduction and supporting a favorite charity, you are able to enhance the annual cash flow from your investment.

3. It is also appropriate for individuals around 60 years old as they prepare for retirement.

Deferred Gift Annuities

A deferred gift annuity works in a similar fashion to a regular charitable gift annuity except you are deferring the start of the annuity payments.

How It Works

Without repeating the mechanics of the charitable gift annuity, here are some additional important features of establishing a deferred gift annuity.

1. The charity will have use of your funds until you begin receiving your annuity payments. Consequently, the power of compounding will have a direct impact on the value of your future annuity.

2. The calculation of your annuity is a factor of your age, the timing of your initial payment, and the discount rate used.

3. Likewise, the above factors will also have a direct impact on the value of your current income tax deduction. The charity will calculate that for you. The younger you are when establishing this gift, the greater your current tax deduction, as you might expect. Your tax deduction also takes place in the year the gift is made.

Advantages

1. Because the annuity begins in the future, your payment will be higher when it begins later than it would be if the annuity started today. Additionally, your current income tax deduction could be quite high (50 percent to 60 percent of the gift), depending on your age.

2. To a certain extent, a deferred annuity acts as a hedge on a single stock position. Your annuity and tax deductions are set at inception, so the value essentially freezes at that point as far as you are concerned.

3. Additionally, your capital gain is deferred over a long time period.

Disadvantages

1. You give up the use of funds for some time in the future.

2. The flip side of hedging your single stock value is that you forgo the benefit of any future appreciation and what that could do for your future cash flow.

Who uses this vehicle?

The deferred gift annuity is essentially a quasi-retirement vehicle. Like traditional retirement plans, the gift annuity compounds tax-free until you begin receiving annuity payments. Generally, your payments begin at or near retirement. It is therefore appropriate for someone who wants to benefit a specific favorite charity while realizing a current income tax deduction coupled with an annuity near retirement.

Pooled Income Funds

As another vehicle to accommodate donors who may not have (or wish to commit) the funds to establish a private foundation or charitable trust, many charities have initiated pooled income funds. Generally, you can enter a pooled income fund with a minimum gift of $10,000, and some funds allow gifts of lower amounts. Not all charities offer this option because of the administrative costs to establish and operate it.

How It Works

Here are some of the highlights of pooled income funds, along with an illustration:

1. Its operation is similar to that of mutual funds: You contribute assets to a commingled fund that includes assets of other donors. For your investment or contribution, you receive a certain number of units reflective of the proportionate value of your contribution to the total funds. You then receive an annual distribution of earned income. However, unlike a mutual fund, the pooled income fund distributes only earned income (and perhaps short-term capital gains), while capital gains remain an asset of the fund. Essentially, it operates as a complex (split-interest) trust when distributing income.

2. You, the donor, will receive actual earned income, as opposed to a stated annuity. Accordingly, the income received will fluctuate over time. Pooled income funds generally offer investment options that include high income, balanced, growth, or aggressive growth funds. The income you receive will be treated as ordinary income for tax purposes.

3. The fund will pay income for your lifetime but can be extended for your spouse's lifetime, as well. If you include someone other than your spouse, you will be making a gift and could be subject to gift

taxes. At your death or your spouse's death, the funds are removed from the pooled income fund and turned over to the charity.

4. The funds remain separate from the general funds of the charity.

5. You are somewhat restricted as to the type of assets you can contribute. Essentially, cash and marketable securities are accepted, with the exception of municipal bonds, which are prohibited by federal statute. Also, non-income producing assets, as well as less liquid assets (such as closely held stock and real estate), are not permitted by most funds. Most funds like to operate as close to a mutual fund as possible and do not want difficult assets.

6. When establishing your interest, you receive an immediate charitable income tax deduction. As with charitable gift annuities, the individual charity will calculate that number for you. The components of this deduction include:

   • Your age and the age of any survivor income beneficiary

   • Value of your contribution

   • Highest rate of return earned by the fund over the past three years. If the fund did not exist for three years, federal guidelines determine this rate.

   The process involves calculating the present value of the charitable remainder interest; this represents your tax-deductible contribution. We illustrate this process below.

7. As expected, this asset will be removed from your taxable estate.

8. If you contribute low-basis stock, there will be no taxable capital gain to you, either now or in the future.

Illustration

You are planning to contribute *$200,000 of your company stock* to a pooled income fund maintained by your local hospital. Your *cost basis in the stock is $50,000*. You are *63 years old*. The highest return on the pooled income fund over the past three years was *7 percent*. Here is a brief illustration of how your tax deduction is calculated:

1. We first calculate the annuity factor for an individual of 63 and an expected return on an investment of 7 percent. From the "Single Life Annuity Factor" table, that number is 9.3767.

2. As this number represents the life interest, we convert it to the charitable remainder interest factors as follows:

   $1 - (9.3767 \times 7\%) = 0.3436$

3. We then multiply this remainder factor by $200,000 to arrive at $68,720. This represents the charitable income tax deduction.

4. Your lifetime income interest is accordingly the difference from $200,000 or $131,280.

Advantages

1. You can make a meaningful gift to a favorite charity without going through the expenses of a private foundation or charitable trust.

2. The variable nature of the income provides an opportunity for a growing asset balance and cash flow, should the fund appreciate in future years.

3. You incur no capital gains tax, either on the initial contribution or on future distributions. It is therefore a good vehicle for some of your appreciated stock holdings.

Disadvantages

1. Your annual income may end up being far less than you might receive on a charitable gift annuity.

2. The benefits of a growth in the asset base are attractive, but beyond your control to influence.

3. As mentioned earlier, many charities do not offer these vehicles. They have enjoyed mixed popularity among non-profit organizations and are costly to operate unless the asset base is significant.

4. Like gift annuities, the fund cannot be split among charities.

Who uses this vehicle?

Pooled income funds work well in at least three situations:

- You are at least 50-55 years old and wish to support a particular charity at your death. However, you want to continue earning current income on some asset pool.

- You have low-basis stock and wish to contribute it to charity without incurring capital gains tax, either currently or on a deferred basis.

- You either do not have the required assets or do not wish to commit the necessary assets to establish a charitable trust or private foundation. You may also have the assets but do not want to incur the expenses of operating a trust or foundation.

THREE

CHARITABLE TRUSTS

One of the more popular techniques for tax and estate planning involves the use of charitable trusts. Generally, trusts are used when larger dollar amounts are committed and, compared to the lifetime gifts just covered, offer wider flexibility in terms of estate and tax planning, as well as asset management. Like traditional complex trusts, charitable trusts are split-interest trusts where there is a current income (or annuity) beneficiary and a remainder beneficiary. One of these beneficiaries is a charity, while the other is usually the grantor, a spouse, or some other individual. Where an individual receives the current annuity or unitrust payment and the charity gets the future remainder interest, the structure is known as a charitable remainder trust. Conversely, where the charity receives the annual annuity or unitrust payment, the trust is known as a charitable lead trust. We will consider each in this chapter. As with the lifetime gifts, we will examine how each works, its advantages and disadvantages, and for whom it best applies. Additionally, we will provide appropriate illustrations.

CHARITABLE REMAINDER TRUSTS

Charitable reminder trusts can be further delineated between annuity or unitrusts. Our analysis will consider each separately, even though there are many common elements between them:

Charitable Remainder Annuity Trusts

In this structure, the trust pays you (and a surviving spouse, if you elect) a stated percentage, translated into dollars, of the initial fair market value of the trust. At termination, the trust then pays the remaining funds to a designated charity.

How It Works

1. The trust can last to cover your lifetime (and your spouse's, if you elect) or for a term not to exceed 20 years.

2. The annual fixed annuity payment to you must be paid annually and cannot be less than 5 percent or greater than 50 percent of the initial value.

3. For a trust of this kind to be valid, there needs to be a fair likelihood that something is left over for the charity. Accordingly, the IRS mandates that the present value of the charitable remainder interest must be at least 10 percent of the initial fair market value.

4. No additional contributions can be made to a specific trust, although you can create additional trusts.

5. The trust must always remain an annuity trust; you cannot change the payout to some other form.

6. Upon creating the trust, you are entitled to an immediate income tax deduction equal to the value of the charitable remainder interest. Factors that contribute to this value include your age, term of the trust, the annual annuity payout, and the relevant IRS discount rate (Section 7520 rate). For example, the longer the trust is expected to run, the lower the charitable remainder interest and, accordingly, the lower your charitable income tax deduction. Also, the higher the annual payout, the lower the tax deduction.

7. Also related to the applicability of an income tax deduction is the so-called "5 percent probability test." In a ruling (Revenue Ruling 77-374), the IRS subjects charitable remainder trusts to a test whereby there cannot be a greater than 5 percent actuarial probability that the trust will be exhausted before the charity receives its money. If the probability of exhaustion is greater than 5 percent, you lose the current income tax deduction.

8. Estate and gift taxes may come into play where any annuity beneficiary is someone other than you or your spouse.

9. The trust itself is not a taxable entity, but you will be directly taxed on the distributions as they occur. There is also a four-tier system of taxable distributions, but we will cover this completely in Chapter 8 on investment management.

Illustrations

Putting the concept into action, let's assume you wish to establish a $2,000,000 charitable annuity trust (using low-basis company stock) under the following operating assumptions:

Your current age: 57

Annual annuity rate: 7 percent

Annual dollar annuity: $140,000

Payment frequency: Semi-annually

IRS Section 7520 rate: 5 percent

Term of annuity: Your life

Remainder interest payable: Local hospital

Complete the charitable remainder interest as follows:

1. Calculate the single-life annuity factor based on age 57 and a 5 percent federal rate. Using the tables, this value is 12.6313.

2. Adjust the annuity factor to account for the annuity's semiannual payment. Using the Annuity Adjustment Factors Table, this number is 1.0123.

3. Calculate the present value of the annuity steam by multiplying the semiannual payments times the annuity factor, times the adjusted factor, as illustrated:

$$\$70,000 \times 2 \times 12.6313 \times 1.0123 = \$1,790,133$$

4. To then arrive at the charitable remainder interest and your income tax deduction, subtract $1,790,133 from your initial $2,000,000 contribution. As a result, you will receive a $209,867 current income tax deduction for setting up this trust.

In Figure 1, we show this precise transaction more schematically. As you see, in addition to the income tax deduction, you also receive a $140,000 fixed annual annuity.

Advantages

1. You can achieve an immediate income tax deduction and do not pay capital gains taxes upon contributing appreciated securities to the trust. Instead, the tax is paid on a tiered basis when funds are distributed.

Figure 1

Charitable Remainder Annuity Trust

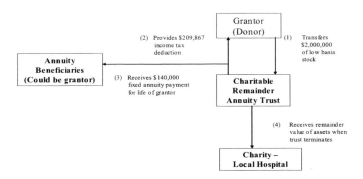

2. You have control over the investment management of the funds, subject to rules on what assets may be included in these trusts. This permits you to contribute and sell a low-yielding asset and then reinvest to achieve higher income.

3. You can select among multiple charitable beneficiaries, unlike the case of charitable gift annuities and pooled income funds.

4. You can determine your annual payment percentage within a wide range (5 percent to 50 percent) instead of having to comply with specific rules of each charity when establishing gift annuities.

5. You receive a fixed annual payment even if the value of the trust or the income drops in a given year.

Disadvantages

1. This is an irrevocable trust.

2. The dollar annuity cannot change. If the value of the trust increases substantially, you will still receive the initially calculated annuity payment.

3. No entity guarantees the annuity. If your investments go bad, you could be out of luck.

4. Operating costs are higher, and administrative burdens are greater than with the lifetime gift options.

5. If the trust's term is based on life expectancy and the donor dies earlier than expected, more of the family funds may end up with charity than desired.

6. For younger people, charities would need to wait a longer time to receive their funds, so other structures are more suitable.

Who uses this vehicle?

1. As already illustrated, this structure fits well with individuals who hold appreciated securities.

2. It is especially attractive during the year when your company is sold and you may have other significant income. The charitable income tax deduction can take some of the sting out of your projected income tax payments.

3. The trust also provides a way to diversify your total exposure to a large, concentrated equity holding. By establishing the trust and selling the stock, you can create a lower-risk asset base from which to support your annual annuity payment. From a total wealth standpoint, you become better diversified; therefore, it is one way to achieve diversification for someone who wants to accomplish that.

4. If you are an insider or control person and are subject to the restricted stock rules (144 and 145), you do not have a constructive sale until the stock is sold within the trust. Accordingly, you do not have to liquidate your entire holding immediately and report sales only when they take place within the trust. However, you may need to report the transfer of the stock to the trust as a gift.

5. As a further wealth transfer technique, the trust can be an effective way to support a second-marriage spouse for life and then benefit a designated charity.

Charitable Remainder Unitrust

Technically following the same split-interest pattern as the charitable remainder annuity trust (CRAT), the charitable remainder unitrust (CRUT) also pays an annual annuity to a non-charitable person while providing the remainder assets to a designated charity. However, the annual payment is a variable annuity based on a stated percentage of the fair market value of the trust, revalued annually. There are some other differences between the CRAT and the CRUT and we will highlight some of them below.

How It Works

1. First, let's summarize some of the features the CRAT and the CRUT have in common:

   - The annual annuity percentage, while applied to a variable asset base, is still 5 percent to 50 percent.

   - The trust may last for the lifetime of individuals or for a term certain of 20 years.

   - The percent value of the charitable remainder interest is still 10 percent. This covers both the initial value and additions.

   - The charitable income, estate, and gift tax rules generally apply, although some of the inputs come from different tables.

   - The annual distribution may come not only from income generated, but also from principal.

2. Unlike the CRAT, the CRUT offers three distribution alternatives:

   - *Net Income Charitable Remainder Unitrust (NICRUT)*

     Under this arrangement, the annual unitrust payout can be the lesser of the unitrust percentage or the actual net income earned during the year. This way, the trustee does not have to invade principal, which could be attractive if you fund the trust with low-trading volume or closely held stock.

   - *Net Income Make-Up Charitable Remainder Unitrust (NIMCRUT)*

     In this case, you also receive the lesser of the stated unitrust percentage or the actual net income generated. However, there is a provision whereby you can make up prior short falls when the actual net income fell short of the unitrust amount. Accordingly, to the extent that the present net income exceeds the unitrust percentage, you can distribute funds to make up for prior shortfalls. This can be attractive when low-yielding assets are sold years later and then reinvested to produce more income.

   - *Flip Unitrust*

     This is actually a combination of all the above. It starts out as either a NICRUT or NIMCRUT and then changes (flips) to a straight CRUT upon a triggering event specified in the governing trust instrument. The triggering event must be something that is beyond the direct control of the donor, beneficiary, or trustee. Also, the "flip" can occur only once and is generally triggered upon such events as marriage, death, birth, or sale of difficult-to-market assets. For the executive or insider, the triggering event could also be the removal of the restriction (Rule 144) on his or her stock. The conversion then allows you to receive a full unitrust distribution even if the trustee is required to sell assets to provide it to you.

With each alternative (NICRUT or NIMCRUT), any pre-contribution capital gain cannot be allocated to distributed income. Post contribution gain can, if provided for in the trust document.

3. With a unitrust, you can add assets after the trust is established, including certain retirement funds.

4. The CRUT itself is not a taxable entity and follows the same process as that of a CRAT, where the donor pays taxes on distributions based on a four-tier system. We will cover this in Chapter 8, when we discuss investment management.

Illustration

We will again show you an example of how the concept works and how your tax deduction is computed. We will illustrate a straight CRUT under the following assumptions:

Contribution: $2,000,000

Your current age: 60

Unitrust payout rate: 6 percent

Payment frequency: Semiannually

IRS Section 7520 Rate: 5 percent

Term: Your life

Remainder interest payable: Local college

We compute the remainder interest as follows:

1. We first adjust the annuity payout factor using the appropriate tables. Incorporating the IRS expected growth rate of 5 percent, coupled with semiannual payments, yields an adjustment factor of 0.964141.

2. Multiplying 0.964141 by the 6 percent unitrust payout results in an adjusted payout rate of 5.7848.

3. We then use the annuity tables (Single Life Unitrust Remainder Factors) to arrive at the appropriate unitrust remainder factor. Rounding up the adjusted payout rate to 5.8 percent, we derive a remainder factor of 0.34257 for an individual 60 years old.

4. Multiplying the remainder factor by the gift results in the following remainder interest:

$$\$2,000,000 \times 0.34257 = \$685,140$$

Your current income tax deduction is \$685,140. This transaction is displayed in Figure 2.

Figure 2
Charitable Remainder Unitrust

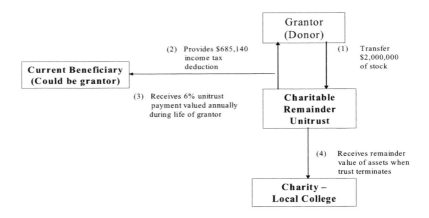

Advantages

1. The CRUT has most of the advantages the CRAT features, including a current income tax deduction, variable payouts, investment flexibility, multiple charitable beneficiaries, and a downside price hedge when you sell a concentrated position.

2. The CRUT, however, offers additional flexible benefits. First, you can add assets once established, unlike a CRAT. An attractive addition could be an IRA or other retirement vehicles that are subject to high taxation at death.

3. The CRUT has multiple income options via the NICRUT, NIMCRUT, and flip unitrust. These features enable you to contribute low-income assets initially, sell them later, and realize high income in years when you may need it more.

4. If you invest successfully and the asset base grows substantially, your payment will correspondingly increase as the unitrust is revalued annually.

Disadvantages

1. Like a CRAT, the CRUT is irrevocable once established. No entity guarantees its continued payout, and operating costs are higher than for gift annuities. Also, if the donor dies prematurely, then more family funds than anticipated could go to charity.
2. Unlike a CRAT, the payout can decrease if the asset base depreciates.

Who uses this vehicle?

While the CRUT applies to the same individuals as a CRAT would, the CRUT again covers a wider universe because of its added flexibilities. For example, if you contemplate adding assets over the years, the CRUT is the right vehicle, particularly if some of those assets are qualified retirement plans. Some of the CRUT variations also fit neatly with certain portfolio issues. Let's take the executives that have restricted stock (subject to Rules 144 and 145). Contributing it to a NIMCRUT or flip CRUT gives them the tax deduction, but also allows them to hold the stock in the trust until it is suitable to sell. They are also not required to liquidate principal to meet any annual payout.

The NICRUT, NIMCRUT, or flip CRUT can also be a neat structure for the investor with real estate. For example, you could contribute real estate to a flip CRUT with the idea you will sell it at a future opportune date and then reinvest the proceeds to support an annuity stream for you and your spouse. All of these techniques are accomplished while providing funds to a charity you wish to support. The CRUT variations are ideal for younger individuals who can wait for a future date to receive full distributions.

CHARITABLE LEAD TRUSTS

In some respects, the charitable lead trust (CLT) is a mirror image of the charitable remainder trust (CRT). Both have a lead income beneficiary and a remainder person. With the charitable lead trust, the designated charity now receives the annual annuity or unitrust payout, while you the donor, your spouse, or some other designated individual receives the remainder interest at the termination of the trust. With the CLT, it is therefore the remainder interest that is now subject to tax and estate planning, and there are many issues and opportunities surrounding it. Another common feature of both the CRT and the CLT is that each has an annuity option, as well as a unitrust option.

Accordingly, our discussion on CLTs will follow the CRT discussion, where we separately view the annuity and unitrust options.

Before proceeding, however, we will look at the two common structural types of charitable lead trusts, as these forms dictate the tax considerations. The first form is the *non-grantor* charitable lead trust, which is the most common one. Some of its important characteristics are:

- You, the grantor, do not receive a current income tax deduction in this situation. At the same time, you are not treated as the owner of the trust for income tax purposes.

- The CLT in this case is a taxable (complex) trust where it is taxed on the income earned, but can offset the income with deductions for funds paid to qualified charities. But any earned income not disbursed will be taxed.

- You can create the trust during your lifetime or at death. If you create the trust at death, your estate receives a charitable estate tax deduction for the lead interest.

- The present value of the remainder interest, if it passes to your heirs, would be considered a completed gift and would be subject to gift taxes to the extent that it exceeds the annual exclusion (currently $11,000) or your lifetime exemption equivalent.

The other CLT form is the *grantor* charitable lead trust, with these general features:

- You can create it only during your lifetime.

- You are considered the owner of the trust for income tax purposes and, as such, are taxed with the income earned by the trust. Accordingly, to the extent possible, municipal bonds are used as a key investment vehicle (to be discussed later in Chapter 8 on investment management).

- On the other hand, you are permitted to receive at inception a charitable income tax deduction equivalent to the present value of the charitable lead unitrust.

- However, if you die before the trust terminates, or if it just ceases to be a grantor trust, the initial charitable income tax deduction is recaptured. The amount of this "recapture" is equal to the initial charitable tax deduction, less the initial present value of the charitable interests that have actually been paid. In essence, you "pay back" to the IRS the value that has not yet been paid to the charity.

- As with the non-grantor trust, the future remainder interest would be a completed gift and could be subject to gift taxes.

Charitable Lead Annuity Trust (CLAT)

With the CLAT, the annuity interest is a fixed amount applied to the initial value of the trust. This fixed-dollar annuity is paid to a qualified charity each year. At termination, the remainder interest is transferred to an individual, usually yourself, your spouse, or your children.

How It Works

1. There is no limit on the specified number of years this trust can last, unlike its CRAT counterpart. Additionally, it can be structured to last the lifetime of individuals living at the time it is created. Furthermore, you could even extend the term of the trust to last a specific lifetime plus a number of years.

2. Also unlike the CRAT, you are not restricted as to the payout percentage. The higher the percentage, however, the lower will be the remainder interest.

3. As with a CRAT, you cannot add assets once the trust is established.

4. Income and appreciation in excess of the required annuity payment can accumulate in the trust for the benefit of the future beneficiaries.

5. Certain types of assets are attractive funding and investment vehicles. Included among those are income-producing securities and assets expected to appreciate. While municipal bonds are attractive from a current income tax perspective, a good dividend-paying stock could also be very suitable since it has a potential growth element.

6. The remainder value is a completed gift, and you must file a gift tax return. The gift also does not qualify for the annual exclusion.

Illustration

As we did with the charitable remainder trusts, we will illustrate how a charitable lead annuity trust actually works. Let's assume the following situation, where your primary motivation is to currently support a local charity while providing what could be a growing remainder interest for your children:

Trust term: 20 years

IRS Section 7520 Rate: 4.6 percent

Trust contribution: $3,000,000

Payout annuity: 6 percent

Payout period: Annually

Annuity amount: $180,000

Trust type: Non-grantor

Term certain annuity factor: 12.8960
Present value of annuity payments: $2,321,280
Remainder interest: $678,720
Charitable interest: Local art museum
Remainder beneficiary: Children
Here is essentially what you accomplish (See Figure 3):

1. You provide your local art museum with an annuity of $180,000 per year for 20 years.

Figure 3
Charitable Lead Annuity Trust
Non-Grantor Trust

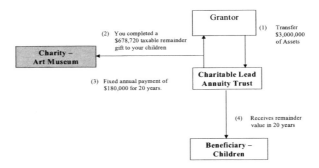

2. Because it is a non-grantor trust, you will not be taxed on the annual income, and the trust will not be taxed so long as it distributes more income than earned.

3. You completed a gift to your children for $678,720, which is equivalent to about one lifetime estate tax exemption. To the extent the remaining assets in the trust exceed $678,720, you will have passed monies to your children estate tax-free.

4. If, on the other hand, you elected to create this as a grantor trust and take a charitable income tax deduction, your deduction would be $2,321,280. However, as mentioned before, you would then be considered the grantor, as well as the taxpayer under the trust. To the extent you have tax-free income, you then defer actual payment of future taxes.

5. The annuity factor of 12.8960 is taken from the Term Certain Annuity Factor tables.

Advantages

1. You have flexibility in selecting the term and the annuity level.

2. You also have both a taxable and a non-taxable option.

3. It can serve as a type of estate "freeze," where you can pass assets to your heirs at no estate tax to the extent you outperform the IRS discount rate used to value the remainder interest.

4. There are no adverse tax consequences if you die before the trust term expires if you have a non-grantor trust.

Disadvantages

1. You cannot add assets to this trust after it is established.

2. Current income tax benefits are not that widespread.

3. You will see later that the CLAT is somewhat disadvantaged as a generation-skipping vehicle.

4. The CLAT itself is not a tax-exempt entity and pays taxes on non-distributed income.

Who uses this vehicle?

With the CLAT, we saw that the current income tax benefits are not as attractive as other techniques. Nevertheless, there are some good financial reasons, beyond the charitable aspects, for creating this type of structure. Among those reasons are the following:

*   In a year when you sell your business for cash or exercise sizeable stock options and are seeking tax deductions, a grantor CLAT may

work out, particularly if you do not need the current income. This gives you the added ability to establish a gift of the remainder interest for your heirs.

- If you have a high-dividend stock and wish to support a charity currently, the CLAT could be a good vehicle for two reasons. First, the dividend could support the annual annuity payments to the charity. Second, if you also expect the stock to appreciate over time, you can build wealth for your heirs, particularly if the stock outperforms the federal discount rate used to value the original annuity and remainder interests.

- The CLAT is especially attractive during low interest rate periods. The low federal discount rates keep the remainder values low. Accordingly, your gift tax exposure is lower, and you have a better chance to beat the federal discount rate. This leaves more assets to your heirs estate tax-free.

- A viable wealth transfer alternative is the *Grantor Retained Annuity Trust,* which has structural elements similar to those of the CLAT. Here you establish a trust for a specified number of years, and you retain the annual annuity interest. The remainder interest passes to your heirs and is considered a taxable gift. If you die before the trust expires, the value of the trust at your death is brought back into your estate and is subject to tax. With a CLAT, the value at death is not brought back into your estate and taxed. Therefore, if you are elderly or in poor health, the CLAT (particularly the non-grantor CLAT) may be a preferred structure to the GRAT (grantor retained annuity trust).

Charitable Lead Unitrust (CLUT)

The charitable lead unitrust (CLUT) is also a vehicle that can be partially used to transfer assets to your children or non-spouses at a reduced estate or gift tax value. The CLUT, like the CLAT, provides a current income stream to a charity for a number of years, with the remaining assets going to your designated heirs.

How It Works

1. As with the CLAT, this trust is not restricted as to term or payout percentage. It also follows the same tax principles as the CLAT, where the remainder value is considered a gift, which does not qualify for the annual exclusion. Also, to the extent that it exceeds your unified credit, there would be potential gift taxes owed. The

value of the gift equals the initial contribution to the CLUT, less the present value of the lead interest to be paid to the charity.

2. Some important differences from the CLAT also exist. The major difference is that the annual payment to charity is based on a fixed percentage of the size of the assets, revalued annually. Consequently, the charitable distributions will fluctuate with the value of the trust.

3. Also, assets may be added to the CLUT; they cannot be added with a CLAT.

Illustration

We will again provide an illustration to show how this structure works. Assume you wish to establish a $3,000,000 CLUT to benefit your alma mater. Consider the following parameters:

Age: 55

Term: 20 years

Percentage payout: 6.0 percent

IRS 7520 Rate: 4.6 percent

Payment period: Semiannual

Remainder beneficiary: Children

In this case, we need to compute the percent value of the remainder interest in order to determine the potential gift taxes. To arrive at this number, we perform these calculations:

1. First, adjust the 6 percent payout for the timing of the unitrust payment. Using the "Unitrust Payout Adjustment Factor" table, we search for the adjustment factor based on a federal 7520 rate of 4.6 percent and semiannual payments. This factor is 0.966894.

2. Multiply this by the payout rate of 6 percent to arrive at an adjusted unitrust payout of 5.8 percent.

3. Find the "term certain unitrust remainder factor" using the appropriate tables. This factor applies to the adjusted payout rate of 5.8 percent and a term of 20 years. The remainder factor is 0.302704.

4. Multiplying this by the value of the gift gives you the remainder interest:

$$\$3,000,000 \times 0.302704 = \$908,112$$

The taxable gift is therefore $908,112. You would owe potential gift taxes to the extent that your available unified credit is exceeded by this value. (See Figure 4.)

Figure 4
Charitable Lead Unitrust
Non-Grantor Trust

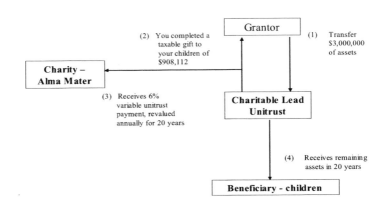

Advantages

1. The CLUT features many of the same advantages as a CLAT, particularly that it can serve as an effective "estate freeze." Income and appreciation in excess of the payout percentage will accumulate in the trust for the benefit of your designated heirs and not be part of your taxable estate.

2. You can add assets to the CLUT. This can be advantageous if, for example, you wish to add future retirement assets or assets at death.

3. As you will see later, the CLUT is an advantageous structure if you wish to leave a remainder interest to your grandchildren. Unlike the CLAT, the CLUT enables the full remainder interest to qualify for the generation-skipping tax exemption.

Disadvantages

1. Taxes are paid on income (to the extent there is taxable income) in a grantor CLT and in a non-grantor trust, there would be no current income tax deduction upon creating the trust.

2. The ability to generate additional wealth for your remainder heirs is not as great with a unitrust (CLUT) as it is with an annuity trust (CLAT). As the value of the unitrust increases (above the federal

rate), the charity gets a greater payment as you revalue the asset base upon which the unitrust payment is made. On the other hand, with the annuity trust (CLAT), the payment is fixed, and any appreciation above the expected discount rate effectively goes to the remainder heirs.

3. As with a CLAT, you lose permanent use of the assets.

Who uses this vehicle?

Again, you would use this structure in many of the same circumstances as you would use the CLAT. There are, however, some particular circumstances where you might favor the CLUT:

- Where you are sure you will want to add assets in the future.

- Where you have a relatively high dividend-paying stock with good appreciation potential. This will enable you to obtain additional wealth for your heirs and, at the same time, generate increasing cash flow for your designated charity.

- If your remainder heirs are your grandchildren, you will want to choose this over the CLAT, as the CLUT can take full advantage of the generation-skipping tax exemption, and the CLAT cannot.

ADMINISTRATION OF CHARITABLE TRUSTS

When contributing assets to charitable gift annuities or pooled income funds, you incur no ongoing administrative tasks, as the respective charities invest the funds, handle tax reporting, and process distributions. On the other hand, when creating charitable trusts, you incur a series of ongoing responsibilities. Here are some of the things you will need to do or have done by someone else.

Create the Trust Document

Charitable trusts are governed by a legal document, which you would engage your attorney to draft. The document spells out such provisions as funding amount, type of trust (annuity or unitrust), trustees, frequency of annuity or unitrust payments, governing law, charitable beneficiary or remainder beneficiary, and investment restrictions, if any. Sample trust documents can be found in *The Tools & Techniques of Charitable Planning* by Stephan R. Leimberg, *et al.*

Select a Trustee

Each trust needs to have a trustee, who will perform most if not all of the administrative duties. Among the potential trustees could be an institutional trust company, the charity receiving the remainder interest, or you, the donor. There are advantages and disadvantages of each. Here are some of the relevant points to consider:

- With an *institutional trustee*, you get the experience and expertise their staff brings to the table, particularly in the areas of tax compliance and investments. On the other hand, their fees range from 75 to 150 basis points, depending on size and investment options. Also, you will need to invest within the parameters of the respective organization.

- You can generally get the *charity* to serve as trustee at a reduced fee, since they are the remainder beneficiary. On the other hand, they may not have the back-office expertise, and you would be required to adopt their investment programs.

- If *you* are trustee, you need to ensure that you do not retain powers that would cause the trust to be disqualified for income tax deduction purposes. An example would be where you can direct the annuity payments in a charitable remainder trust.

Understand Investments

The trustee needs to consider a number of factors when investing, but the two most important ones are the definition of unrelated business income and a clear understanding of the four-tier system of recognizing the tax liability of distributed income. These will be covered in Chapter 8 on investment management.

Ensure Tax Compliance

A critical role for the trustee is to ensure proper and timely filing of tax information and returns. Some of the tax forms that must be filed include:

- Tax Form 5227: Split Interest Trust Information Return
- Tax Form 1041A: U.S. Information Return of Trust Accumulation of Charitable Amounts
- Schedule K-1 of Form 1041: Beneficiary's Share of Income, Deductions, Credits, etc.

There can also be other forms, depending on whether the trust has unrelated business income or violated any private foundation rules, which we cover in the next chapter.

Perform Trustee Duties

The trustee has a range of recordkeeping duties necessary to ensure that proper distributions take place and that assets are properly valued. Among the responsibilities are:

- For charitable unitrusts, calculate the asset value and new annual unitrust payments.

- Distribute regular annuity and investment payments.

- Calculate tax nature of each distribution – ordinary income, capital gains, municipal, and return of capital.

- Maintain principal and income accounting.

- Where a NIMCRUT is involved, keep tack of income paid, along with a running total of income deficits that can be made up in later years.

- Close out and pay remainder beneficiaries when trust terminates.

We emphasized throughout this chapter on charitable trusts that there is a charity that receives either the remainder interest or the lead interest in the trust. These charities can be traditional ones, such as schools, hospitals, and social service organizations. They can also be foundations – private or public. For example, you can establish your own private family foundation or set up a fund at the local community foundation to be the direct beneficiary of the charitable trust's payments. We will now take a look at these and other foundation alternatives.

FOUR

THE WORLD OF FOUNDATIONS

While estate planning and tax deductions are important, you may also want to become more engaged in the world of philanthropy. You may want your children involved and wish to establish a family legacy in your community. If that's you, then you are ready to participate in the field of foundations. We will look at this critical aspect of charitable giving from the following angles:

- We will start with a tour of the world of private foundations, examining its benefits as well as its drawbacks. We will also cover some of its important operating rules.

- Using the private foundation as the baseline structure, we then turn to some alternatives, beginning with community foundations.

- We will explore the features and benefits of donor-advised funds and supporting organizations as further alternatives to establishing a private family foundation. We will focus on when these options can be more feasible.

- Finally, we will comment on corporate foundations and how an overall corporate giving structure can be established.

PRIVATE FAMILY FOUNDATIONS

Strictly speaking, a private foundation is an entity established to make grants to charitable and other qualified non-profit organizations, which then provide services to the public. The foundation itself does not engage directly in providing these services. Additionally, private foundations generally have a single funding source, such as an individual, family, or company. Expenses to operate the foundation come from the income generated on its investments.

Private foundations as we know them today have their genesis with the passage of the Tax Reform Act of 1969. It is here where Congress separated "private" from "public" foundations. This separation was required to correct some earlier abuses and to establish a more proper regulatory structure governing each. Essentially, a private foundation is any foundation that *does not meet any* of the following descriptions:

- A traditional non-profit operation, such as a school, hospital, religious, or governmental organization

- A "gross receipts" organization, such as museums that are support by a broad spectrum of the public

- Supporting organizations designed to support one or a few specific charities

- Public safety organizations

The major differentiating features between public and private foundations lie in the tax deductibility and appraisal of contributed assets, as well as the ongoing operating rules and procedures, along with penalties for non-compliance.

When Do You Establish a Private Foundation?

A fundamental question is when an individual or family should think about establishing a full-fledged foundation. It makes sense when several of these circumstances exist:

- First, you should use other structures if the committed assets are going to be less than $1 million; some experts will tell you the funding should be at least $3 million or $5 million. Two important exceptions exist to this guideline.

  - Many foundations are established under the will of individuals, so the major funding takes place at death. It is sometimes a good idea to establish the foundation while you are alive, even if it is small, so you can put its structure in place and see that it operates according to your intentions.

  - A second exception is where you use the foundation as a flow-through entity to receive assets and distribute them over a short period of time. This approach is common when you hold real estate and may wish to sell it before contributing the funds to your foundation. Many corporate foundations work like this.

- You have and are willing to contribute significant assets to charity, but other structures do not afford the same level of tax deductibility.

- You wish to support many different charities and need a structure for evaluating proposals, processing grants, and reviewing performance of the grantees.

- You have decided to leave your children a finite pool of money and not more. A foundation is an effective tax-free way to dispose of the remainder.

- You are attracted to the idea of having a vehicle that could bring together family members in a worthwhile cause. The foundation can also serve as a forum to educate the younger family members on the virtues and processes of community giving.

- You want to leave a lasting imprint on your community and wish to have future generations remain among its philanthropic leaders.

- Finally, you want direct control on the process. Specifically, you want to decide how the funds are invested and how the grants are selected.

How Do You Establish a Private Foundation?

Once you determine you want to establish a private foundation, you now have to go through the various legal steps to actually set it up. You will need legal counsel to formally establish the foundation, as the regulatory authorities require several forms of documentation. Here is a synopsis of some of the steps involved:

1. Determine Foundation Type

A foundation can take one of two legal forms. You can establish it as a trust or as a non-profit corporation under the laws of the resident state. Under the trust form, your start-up process is less onerous, and your operating procedures are generally less formal. However, trusts are sometimes harder to change and could in some instances require court approval. Trustees usually have more implied liability than corporate directors. The governing document is a formal trust agreement.

Under the corporate form, the set-up is a little more involved, and the ongoing operations are more formal. To create the foundation, your attorney will need to draft formal articles of incorporation and bylaws, along with other particular state filings that might be required. The corporate structure is sometimes formed because of its greater flexibility to handle changes in the future. For instance, the bylaws can deal easily with the succession and removal of officers and directors; whereas, it is sometimes harder to remove trustees. You also have more implied ability and powers to alter the foundation's mission to adapt to changing times and circumstances. Finally, some states provide a safer harbor to indemnify officers and directors under the corporate form of organization.

2. *Tax Filings*

To achieve legal status as a tax-exempt entity, the foundation needs to file Form 1023 with the Internal Revenue Service, "Application for Recognition of Exemption Under Section 501©3 of the Internal Revenue Code." This form gets you your tax-exempt status. In addition to this action, you would file Form 872-C (dealing with excise tax), Form SS-4 (to get an employer identification number), and Form 709 (to report the gift of assets upon funding). Then, on an annual basis you file a tax information return called Form 990-F, and for your employees you would issue 1099s.

3. *Funding*

You have a variety of sources from which to seed a foundation. First, you can make outright gifts of cash or securities either during your lifetime or under your will. Alternatively, if you establish a charitable remainder trust, your private foundation can receive the remainder assets at the termination of the trust. On the other hand, if you have a charitable lead trust, the annual income can flow to your foundation. There are still other methods, such as insurance, retirement assets, and charitable partnerships, which we will cover in later chapters. Figure 5 diagrams some of these traditional alternatives.

4. *Governance*

Once established and funded, a foundation needs to begin operating to fulfill its intended purpose. Some of the important governance issues include:

- Selecting trustees or directors and specifying the number, terms, and class (for example, occupation, family *versus* non-family). Also, specifying the process for succession and removal, as well as compensation, if applicable.

- Determining the specific board and management officers. Outlining the process for election and removal.

Figure 5
Ways to Fund Your Private Foundation

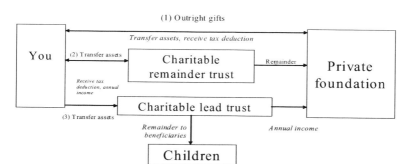

- Determining which board committees are necessary to carry out your activities. Most foundations have a formal selection committee that sets grant-making policies and reviews certain grants, while some of the larger foundations also have formed investment committees to oversee the management of assets.

- Setting in place the controls to ensure that all tax compliance rules are adhered to. In the table on the next two pages, we summarize those important compliance rules.

- Establishing a process for approving grant requests.

- Arranging to make tax returns and other designated records available for public inspection.

- Determining the circumstances under which the foundation might terminate, along with options for disbursing or transferring the funds. Foundations may terminate for a number of reasons. Some will have a term limit in their original charter. Others may have fulfilled their intended mission or goal. Still others may terminate because no family member wants to continue operating them. If that day arrives, you could specify several options for distributing funds, including:

Foundation Tax Compliance Monitoring

Tax	Description	Purpose	Tax/Penalty
Excise Tax on Investment Income (Section 4940)	Tax on net investment income, which includes capital gains. Investment related expenses such as manager fees are deductions from investment income and net capital gains. Net capital losses cannot be carried forward and do not reduce the tax base. Tax paid is allowed as credit against payout requirement.	Pay for cost of auditing and regulating private foundations.	2% of net investment income, but can be reduced to 1% if foundation meets certain payout tests.
Minimum Payout Ratio (Section 4942)	Foundations must meet an annual payout of 5% of their calculated asset value, based on average monthly values of prior year, adjusted for qualifying expenses needed to support grant-making activities.	To ensure that foundations serve their stated purpose.	Penalty of 15% of the shortfall. Foundation has 12 months to make up shortfall to avoid further penalty.
Tax on Self-Dealing (Section 4941)	Private foundations cannot engage in financial transactions with certain "disqualified persons," regardless of price – generally, trustees, directors, staff, and family members. Transactions generally mean buying, selling, or leasing property; lending money; or furnishing goods and services. Trustees and family members can be paid for management services, provided the price is competitively fair.	To prevent conflicts of interest and misuse of foundation assets.	Penalty of 5% of the value of the transaction is assessed to the individual engaged in the self-dealing.
Taxes on Excess Business Holdings (Section 4943)	Private foundations cannot control an operating business and are therefore restricted as to their percent of ownership (either 20% or 35%, based on composition of ownership by disqualified persons).	To prevent advantageous use of tax-exempt status to compete in the commercial marketplace.	Tax of 5% on amount held in excess of limit. Foundation has 5 years to divest donated shares before tax is imposed.
Unrelated Business Income Tax (UBIT-Section 501-A)	Refers to income earned from a trade or business unrelated to foundation's tax-exempt purpose. Could include limited partnership interests and debt-financed properties.	To even the competitive advantages enjoyed by foundations.	Subject to corporate tax rates

Tax	Description	Purpose	Tax/Penalty
Tax on	The IRS frowns on foundations	To protect assets	Tax of 5% on

Jeopardy Investments (Section 4944)	making high-risk investments. They require directors and trustees to exercise prudence in committing funds and will levy penalties if such care is not taken.	of foundations from both high risk and fraudulent investments.	amount of investment is assessed to the foundation, and 5% is assessed on foundation manager who makes the investment.
Tax on Taxable Expenditures (Section 4945)	Regulations cover restrictions on certain types of grants, including lobbying, political contributions, grants to individuals, grants to non-charities, and expenditures for non-charitable purposes, although exceptions to each exist.	To ensure funds are expended in ways that directly benefit charitable or non-profit organizations.	Tax of 10% on amount involved, and 2.5% taxed to foundation director.

- Merge with another private foundation.
- Establish a fund at the community foundation or give them the funds outright.
- Distribute the remaining assets. The process can be left to the directors or trustees, or you can specify how you want the funds distributed (for example, to a university, a hospital, or an anti-poverty organization).
- There is also a process whereby you may be able to transform your private foundation to a supporting organization. Generally, unless the original governing instruments specify otherwise, you need to provide a 60-month advance notice if you wish to terminate a foundation (IRS code section 507). There is also a termination tax imposed. One way to avoid the 60-month period and tax is to transfer the foundation assets to a qualified supporting organization through what is called the SOAR technique. Your attorney can guide you through this process.

Benefits of Establishing a Family Foundation

Earlier, we spoke about the reasons to establish a private family foundation. Here are some additional benefits for doing so:

- If you wish to maintain a continuous stream of support for one or several charities, you may find it attractive to transfer funds in years when you have significant income and then reduce transfers in years of lower income. The foundation needs to distribute only 5 percent of the principal annually. You receive the income deduction, within IRS limitations, in the year you contribute it. Accordingly, the foundation provides flexibility in funding, as well as distributions.

- You can establish an effective buffer between yourself and the charities submitting proposals.

- In some instances, you can coordinate the programs of your company's foundation with your family foundation to better leverage gifts.

- Unless the governing documents are highly restrictive, the foundation, particularly the corporate form, is flexible enough that you can revise its mission to meet the changing needs of the community.

- Within strict guidelines, you can employ family members as officers of the foundation. This can provide an excellent forum for your family to participate in the affairs of your community.

Drawbacks to Establishing a Foundation

A foundation sounds great, but it does have its drawbacks. Some of these shortcomings can be alleviated through alternative structures, which we will discuss below. Accordingly, here are some of those drawbacks:

- The cost of setting up a foundation can be high. You will need attorneys to draft governing documents and to execute appropriate filings with the IRS and state authorities. However, if the size of your foundation is large enough to warrant these expenses, you should not be deterred, since these costs will be low relative to the activities of the entity.

- Ongoing administration is far more involved than for alternative entities. You need to ensure that all IRS tax compliance guidelines and rules are followed. Also, you need to handle the grant-making process, which can be involved for many foundations.

- As we discuss later, the tax deductibility rules are not as liberal for private foundations as they are for other structures.

- If you want to contribute closely held business stock, there are several complications, including the general inability to obtain a tax deduction based on current fair market value.

ALTERNATIVE STRUCTURES

Today there are more than 50,000 private family foundations in the United States, so the concept is indeed popular. Furthermore, foundations are key players in civic affairs in all major communities across the country. But, still within the spirit of foundations, some alternative structures enable you to accomplish many of the same things if you are willing to relinquish varying degrees of control. We will turn to those now.

Donor Advised Funds

Fast becoming the most popular alternative to the private foundation is the donor advised fund. By definition, the donor advised fund is a charitable program established at a public charity, from which distributions go to qualified charitable recipients. Traditionally, the hosting public charities have been local community foundations, but in recent years, financial institutions that sponsor mutual fund complexes have established them. Some of the well known institutions are Bank of America, Northern Trust, T. Rowe Price, and Fidelity, which was perhaps the first to enter this field.

When financial institutions offer donor advised funds, they generally partner with an independent public charity to administer the philanthropic piece. Examples are community foundations or such national entities as the National Philanthropic Trust, which specializes in administering donor advised funds. Still other institutions, such as universities, are beginning to establish their own donor advised funds in an effort to get their donors' monies closer to their institution. Regardless of where your fund is housed, there are two important components to these vehicles. First, they are permanently endowed funds that are pooled with other participants' monies. Second, you may advise the charity as to distributions, but your recommendations are non-binding.

When do you use these?

Donor advised funds look very much like private foundations. In fact, many call them the "poor man's foundation." Size does have a role in deciding what vehicle to use, but there are also many other factors, including:

- In addition to size considerations, you also want a foundation-like structure that is less costly to establish and less involved to operate.

- As with a foundation, you want to be able to time your contributions and distributions more precisely. For example, in years when you have high income or liquidate low-basis holdings, you will seek tax deductions and may wish to contribute a large amount to a charitable vehicle. On the other hand, you may not want it all distributed then and may not even know how much you ultimately want to give to any charity. The donor advised route can well accommodate you, since you receive the income tax deduction in the year funds are distributed to the fund, not when the fund distributes monies to the qualified charities. There are income limitations, however, and we will go over those in a subsequent chapter.

- You may need to set up a fund quickly at year-end.
- In addition to your company stock, you may also have a number of other low-basis positions you might want to use as funding vehicles, but wish to do so over a number of years.
- You want a vehicle in which your family members, such as children and even grandchildren, can become involved in selecting grantees.
- You want flexibility in choosing grantees and the ability to change direction at any time.
- You have a few very specific organizations you want to support with meaningful gifts in the future. You presently do not have the level of funds you want to contribute. For example, let's say you wish to donate $2 million in company stock to the University of Texas to endow a chair in physics. You have only about half of the available funds today and hope to be in a position to fund the chair in about ten years. Instead of waiting, you can establish a donor advised fund today for $1 million and invest it in a tax-free environment for ten years. This way, you may be able to earn the monies needed in a shorter period of time.
- You want to do something with your IRA, realizing that when you leave it to your children, it will be highly taxed.

How do you establish a fund?

Once you determine the provider through whom you wish to establish your fund, you generally need to go through the following steps:

1. *Agreement:* Each sponsoring institution will have a formal account agreement you will sign.
2. *Funding:* You determine the type of assets and amount. Generally, you contribute cash and marketable securities, but some funds can facilitate contributions of mutual funds, real estate, and restricted stock. With restricted stock, you will need to follow the rules of your company, and if you are considered an insider, you may need to

report the transfer of stock as a gift. The host charity reserves the right to reject and return any contributed security. It should also be noted that the donor advised fund can be funded through a charitable remainder or a lead trust.

3. *Purpose:* You have the right to name the fund and can outline its purpose.

4. *Investments:* Each host charity will have its own set of investment pools or vehicles. You generally have the right to allocate your monies into those designated funds. Accordingly, you have the ability to control the asset allocation, but not more than that. The actual management of the funds is the responsibility of the charity and its designated investment advisors.

5. *Grant-making:* It is here where the true nature of these vehicles is defined. You, the donor, can recommend where the funds should be distributed, but the charity has the final say. For example, the charity is responsible to ensure that grants go to approved charities qualified under IRS regulations – 501(c)(3) non-profit organizations – approved religious and educational institutions, and certain foreign charities. The charity may also investigate as to whether the grants are for non-approved purposes. Examples include grants to individuals, political parties, or private non-operating foundations. Grants also cannot benefit the donor or the donor's family in any way. You cannot give funds, for instance, to satisfy a pledge you made to a museum or to a college as partial payment of tuition or fees if your child is attending. There is another aspect to grant-making in that you can be asked to specify a particular field of interest. This becomes relevant in case you cease to recommend grants for an extended period of time. The sponsoring charity has the ability then to make grants, but will generally do so in your specified areas of interest.

6. *Fees:* Each sponsoring organization will have its own fee schedule, but you will generally pay separately disclosed fees to cover charitable administration, investment management, and donor servicing.

Additional Advantages

In addition to the reasons for establishing donor advised funds, there are other distinct advantages for using this structure:

- You gain the maximum tax advantages, as we will show in later chapters. You essentially get the tax considerations you would with a gift to a public charity.

- Currently, you are not subject to the 5 percent annual distribution requirement, but it is very likely Congress will mandate this in the future.

- You do not have to file a separate tax return, as you are included in the sponsoring charity's tax filings.

- Your investment income is not subject to the 2 percent excise tax that private foundations pay.

- Even if you have substantial funds you can later allocate to a private family foundation, this can be a good interim structure, as the minimums to establish a fund are very low. They range from $10,000 to $25,000, depending on the charity.

Disadvantages

The donor advised fund almost sounds like a no-brainer, but there are some drawbacks, compared to other vehicles:

- There are sometimes several layers of fees, and each organization will have minimum charges. Therefore, as a percentage of assets, the fees could exceed 2 percent in any given year. The rates, of course, will decrease on a percentage basis as the assets in the fund grow.

- Your investment options are what the charity offers, and you have limited ability to influence them.

- Some charities have internal restrictions on grant amounts.

- Congress is likely to issue additional rules governing these structures.

Selecting a Provider

With the proliferation of providers getting into the donor advised business, how should you go about selecting a provider? While there are no hard and fast rules, you may want to consider these factors:

- Check with your financial adviser or private bank. They may already offer or intend to offer these services. As you are already familiar with their investment management, it may be convenient to establish a fund through them.

- If you intend to give to a known group of charities, you may also prefer a financial institution, as you will not be relying on their charitable expertise and may also not need the charitable expertise of local community foundations.

- On the other hand, if you want to become an active player in the community and want to collaborate with other donors in larger projects, the community foundation option will be the preferred route. They will be in a good position to identify charitable opportunities.

- Needless to say, if you are on the board of the local community foundation or are just very active in philanthropic affairs, you may feel some obligation to support the community foundation.

Supporting Organizations

Suppose you wish to support the local community foundation or an organized religious charity, such as the common Catholic or Jewish federations. You are willing to have a significant portion of your charitable bequests run through these entities. A private foundation may not be the most feasible option in these cases. Furthermore, your assets consist of low-basis, closely held stock, restricted low-basis stock, or real estate. An attractive alternative could be a supporting organization, which is defined as a charitable corporation or trust created in direct affiliation with a specified public charity or charities. As such, it enjoys many of the tax and operating benefits of contributions to public charities. We will first look at how these entities work and then evaluate when they are appropriate.

How do they work?

It can sometimes be complicated to establish a supporting organization, so once again, you should consult with your attorney as to the appropriate process.

As a starting point, you can establish your supporting organization as either a trust or a corporation. In this case, it is sometimes easier to use the trust form because it is less costly to set up and operate. Also, there are three basic types of supporting organizations from which you need to select. This decision defines how the entity will operate. We will consider each:

1. *Type 1 – Controlled:* In this case, the supported charity controls the board and the daily operations, much as a parent corporation controls its subsidiaries. In particular, the charity will appoint all or at least a majority of the board members.

2. *Type 2 – Supervised or controlled in connection with:* Here both the supporting organization and the supported charity are governed by

the same board and/or officers to ensure that the supporting organization is always responsive to the needs of the public charity.

3. *Type 3 – Operated in connection with:* With this entity, the donor has the most control, but there are more restrictions placed on its structure and operations. The idea is that the supporting organization must be responsive to the needs of the charity and integrally part of its operation. There are two tests that the supporting organization must meet to qualify as Type 3: the responsiveness test and the integral part test.

To meet the responsiveness test, there can be common control between the supporting organization and the charity. This control can be in the form of having the charity elect one of the directors or trustees of the supporting organization. Another way is to have the supporting organization established as a charitable trust, have the specific public charities named in the governing trust instrument, and give the public charities the right to ask for formal accountings.

The integral part test can be met by having the supporting organization perform certain functions that the public charity would ordinarily perform. For example, you can allow the charity to use assets, such as land or facilities, to carry out its work, assuming a significant role in the operations. Another way to meet this test is to distribute 85 percent of the income to the public charity.

There are still two other requirements or tests that all types of supporting organizations must pass. The first is the Organizational and Operations test, which is described in section 509(a)(3)(A) of the Internal Revenue code. The purpose of this test is to ensure that the supporting organization carries out activities that fully support the public charity and does not stray into non-charitable activities. Any independent grants must also support the mission of the public charities it was set up to support.

The second test is the Control test, which is described under section 509 (a)(3)(C) of the Internal Revenue code. Its purpose is to ensure that the donor, family members, or any entity controlled by the donor does not control the supporting organization. As Type 1 and Type 2 organizations take care of the control issue, we are just dealing here with Type 3 organizations. Essentially, these disqualified persons cannot have more than 50 percent of the board seats and cannot control how the distributions are allocated.

Why have supporting organizations become so popular?

Particularly among business owners and executives, this structure has been growing in popularity. Among the reasons are taxes, foundation regulations, and the range of contributed assets, as explained here:

- Because you are contributing to a public charity, you can realize the maximum income tax deductions for charitable giving. We will cover these specifics in Chapter 6.

- It is perhaps the most appealing structure for contributing closely held stock, restricted stock, and real estate. First, the supporting organization will generally accept these assets. Second, with a supporting organization, you may be required to distribute only 85 percent of the earned income in any given year, not the 5 percent distribution required of private foundations. Accordingly, you will not be under pressure to sell assets to meet the payout requirements. The assets can remain in the trust and, it is hoped, appreciate for some future charitable use.

- You are also not subject to other private foundation rules. In particular, there is no 2 percent excise tax on investment income.

- Another set of private foundation rules does not apply, and these are critical for holders of restricted stock, closely held stock, and real estate. These rules encompass self-dealing limitations, excess business holdings, and jeopardy investments. As a result, with a supporting organization, you can hold a concentrated position of a closely held business or a large track of real estate. This would otherwise be in violation of fiduciary investment standards if you held these in a private foundation.

- Even though you give up control to a governing board, you and your family are able to maintain positions on the board and can still influence, but not control, decisions.

- When you establish these structures, you are not limited to supporting just one public charity. However, you are likely to support just a couple so that you can have an impact.

Considerations

While there are many advantages to supporting organizations, there are also some issues to consider before establishing them:

- The gift is irrevocable, and if you are an insider, you may need to report it.

- You must name the supported public charities when you set up the structure and cannot add others later.

- Even though you escape some of the IRS tax compliance rules of private foundations, you do have other regulations specific to supporting organizations, particularly with Type 3 organizations.

- The costs of establishing supporting organizations can be similar to those of private foundations and are probably higher than donor advised funds.

- Ongoing compliance monitoring is important, particularly as it relates to activities with the donor and other disqualified persons. Also, even though your annual payout requirement is low, you should always carefully assess whether you are fulfilling your original charitable intent.

Private Operating Foundations

Taking the private foundation and supporting organization concepts further, you can also establish what is called a private operating foundation. This entity does not make grants to other charities; instead, it conducts the actual charitable activities itself. For example, it will operate a museum or a soup kitchen or hire staff directly to do that. To qualify as a private operating foundation, the entity must devote a significant amount of its income and assets to the intended purpose. We will not cover the particulars here but wanted to mention it as a further alternative. We should also note that contributions to fund these structures would provide the maximum tax advantages, as they would be considered gifts to a public charity.

Community Foundations

We spoke frequently about community foundations and how you can use them to structure and carry out your charitable plans. In particular, they play an important role in the donor advised fund and supporting organization markets. Therefore, we will take a moment to discuss these important organizations in their own right.

Community foundations are defined as tax exempt, philanthropic institutions consisting of funds that have been permanently endowed by many donors for the purpose of supporting a defined local community. They are governed by a board of directors representing a broad cross section of community philanthropists and leading citizens.

Community foundations can be set up in either a trust or a corporate form. If the trust form is used, you would have a local bank serve as the corporate trustee.

A community foundation operates four common types of funds:

1. *Unrestricted funds* are, as you would expect, the most sought after because they give the foundation staff full discretion to allocate the monies in accordance with the most pressing community needs at the time.

2. *Designated funds* enable you to select the specific charitable beneficiary to receive the funds. You generally do this at the time you create the fund.

3. *Donor advised funds* are, as we mentioned earlier, one of fastest growing vehicles. This structure gives the donor the ability to recommend charitable recipients, but the community foundation has the final decision. The foundation, however, generally goes along with the donor's recommendations.

4. *Field of interest funds* are available to individuals who are interested in a specific cause or type of institution, but who are willing to let the community foundation select the actual recipients. These funds also make it easier for the community foundation to continue on after your death.

Another feature about community foundations is relevant for your planning. Community foundations have what is called a "variance power." This power enables them to change or modify any established restrictions in the future. It can do so if the original mandate becomes obsolete or impossible to fulfill. Consider, for instance, a designated fund wherein one of the recipients is a nursing home and hospital. The institution closes, and its assets are distributed to satisfy remaining debts. You can no longer provide funds to this entity, so you would naturally need to redirect the funds.

When do you consider a community foundation option?

Community foundations can be used as either your primary charitable vehicle or one of several in your overall program. Here are some of the reasons for considering an affiliation with your local community foundation:

- You and your company are among the leading philanthropists in the community, and you want to show support for the community foundation so others will follow.

- You want to become more active in the philanthropic community but do not wish to go through the paperwork to set up and operate your own foundation.
- You want to be somewhat insulated from a barrage of grant proposals.
- You want some perpetual management of your philanthropic funds with the ability to change course when needed.

Corporate Foundations

Before concluding this chapter on foundations, we will say a word about your company's giving structure. There are several ways your company can structure its charitable giving; here are a few of them:

- You can still just write a check from your current year's earnings. Companies can deduct up to 10 percent of their current earnings for charitable contributions.
- You can establish a matching gift program that enables employees to leverage their gifts to their colleges and favorite local charities.
- You can establish a formal foundation. An advantage of doing this is that you can fund an endowment as you go along. In good earning years, you can fund it more, and in lean years, less. This allows your company to continue with its charitable commitments during the lean years when it is likely the charities will also be hurting. Additionally, the foundation gives your company a higher community profile. While the foundation would be subject to many of the tax compliance rules that private foundations face, it generally does not need to worry much about them. The 5 percent annual payout should be easy to achieve, since you are not likely ever to have a huge endowment at any one time. Also, the 2 percent excise tax will be small.

We have now considered most of the traditional charitable structures that would be appropriate alternatives for executives, business owners, and other individuals who hold concentrated assets. Moving on, we will look at some of the more advanced and somewhat creative strategies that expand upon these traditional techniques.

FIVE

ADVANCED CHARITABLE TECHNIQUES

You might think the traditional array of charitable structures gives most of us an ample menu to pick from. Not so. While the analytical process can become complicated, there are many variations to these structures that can enable you to more efficiently weave your philanthropic strategies into your overall wealth transfer plan. Setting up these advanced structures will require assistance from competent legal, tax, and, in some cases, insurance counsel. Accordingly, our intent here is only to alert you to some of the more interesting possibilities in the marketplace. We will not go into as much detail on each as we did with the more traditional techniques, as each must be adapted to your personal circumstances.

Wealth Replacement Trusts

Suppose you like the idea of a charitable remainder trust that will enable you to contribute your low-basis company stock, sell it without paying an immediate capital gains tax, and receive an annuity for life that is much greater than the dividend you currently receive. And at the same time, you'd get a current income tax deduction equivalent to the present value of the charitable remainder interest. One important missing element is that your children or heirs will not get this money. If they are in a position to get other significant funds, then you are probably okay. But if you are beginning to doubt whether they will have enough funds after your death, there is an option.

At the time you establish the CRT, you would set up an irrevocable life insurance trust funded by a policy that will provide an adequate inheritance for your heirs. The premiums will be paid from a portion of the annuity you receive from the CRT. Figure 6 illustrates how the insurance trust fits into the overall program.

Figure 6
Wealth Replacement Trusts

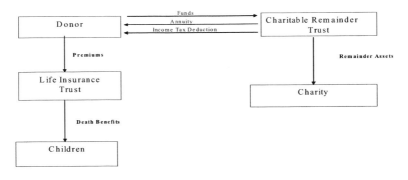

Short-term (Accelerated) Charitable Remainder Trusts

If you recall, a charitable remainder trust can have an annual payout of between 5 percent and 50 percent. While they are usually set up for longer time periods, you can establish them to pay out more quickly. There are certain instances when you might want to do this. One would be when you want to use the funds in a new business venture. You may have just sold your company for stock and wish to use the CRT to achieve the immediate tax deduction and fulfill certain charitable obligations in a short time period. At the same time, you know there is an opportunity to invest in a new company over the next couple of years, and you'd like to have the capital back to do so. By setting up the CRT to pay out over three or five years, you can achieve all of your short-term objectives while staying well within the IRS guidelines. As to the charity, it could have immediate capital needs and might enjoy receiving any funds earlier rather than later.

Short-term charitable remainder trusts can also be incorporated within more complex estate planning structures. For example, you can combine them with family limited partnerships, insurance, and dynasty trusts to transfer wealth to succeeding generations in a tax efficient manner. The process is quite involved and should be discussed with your tax advisers, but here is an example of a transaction:

1. Start by creating a family limited partnership, funding it with $3 million of income-producing investment real estate and $7 million of marketable securities, which could include your company stock. As a quick definition, a family limited partnership is a limited-liability structure created under the laws of a particular state. The owners are limited to family members who contribute property in exchange for ownership interests. A general partner, usually the head of the family, manages and controls the entity. The remaining owners are limited partners. Because the units are not transferable outside the family and are also not readily redeemable, there is a valuation discount. This facilitates transfers among family members at a discount, providing attractive wealth transfer possibilities.

2. Next, establish and fund a Delaware Dynasty Trust that would be exempt from generation-skipping transfer (GST) taxes. Each individual has a lifetime GST exemption of around $1 million. The GST tax is levied on transfers that are two or more generations from you. Additionally, the trust would be considered an intentionally defective grantor trust, which means that you, the grantor, would be taxed on the income. These trusts could last in perpetuity or terminate on a designated date, usually far into the future.

3. Then sell your limited partnership units to the dynasty trust on an installment basis. This sale would be clear of capital gains taxes, since the trust is considered a grantor trust for income tax purposes. In other words, you are actually selling the units to yourself.

4. Subsequent to the sale, establish within the family limited partnership a short-term charitable remainder trust, and transfer the $7 million investment portfolio into it. As a result, you and the family limited partnership realize a charitable income tax deduction for the remainder interest going to charity.

5. The trustee of the family limited partnership will use the real estate income to purchase a $25 million second-to-die life insurance policy.

6. During the term of the charitable remainder trust, the annuity proceeds are used to pay off the installment sale note.

7. Finally, upon the death of the surviving spouse, the CRT assets pass to the charity, and the life insurance proceeds go to your heirs to replace those assets.

Zeroed-out CLATs

You will recall from our earlier discussion that the charitable lead annuity trust first provides for an annual annuity payment to a designated charity for a specified number of years and then distributes the remaining assets back to you, your spouse, your heirs, or some other individual. At inception, the present value of the remainder interest is considered a gift and is subject to gift taxes if the remainder beneficiary is someone other than your spouse. This present value is calculated using the Term Certain Annuity Factors tables and is affected by the term and the Federal AFR Rate (Section 7520) discussed earlier.

Consider the situation wherein the present value of the annuity payments to charity are exactly equal to the original funds transferred and thus, the present value of the remainder interest is zero. CLATs structured in this manner are termed "Zeroed-out CLATs," and no gift or very little gift is involved.

Perhaps the best way to visualize this situation is to consider a live example as displayed in the table below. Here we are establishing a $2,000,000 CLAT for a term of ten years. The annual charitable annuity is $246,600, or approximately 12.3 percent. The Federal APR, or discount rate, is 4 percent, meaning the trust is expected to grow at a 4 percent annual rate.

Year	Beginning Balance	Performance Growth (4%)	Annuity Payment	Ending Balance
1	$2,000,000	$80,000	$(246,600)	$1,833,400
2	1,833,400	73,336	(246,600)	1,660,136
3	1,660,136	66,405	(246,600)	1,479,941
4	1,479,,941	59,198	(246,600)	1,292,539
5	1,292,539	51,701	(246,600)	1,097,640
6	1,097,640	43,906	(246,600)	894,946
7	894,946	35,798	(246,600)	684,144
8	684,144	37,366	(246,600)	464,910
9	464,910	18,596	(246,600)	236,906
10	236,906	9,476	(246,600)	(218)

Now consider what happens if the actual investment results exceed the 4 percent expected federal rate, as illustrated in the table below. Here we assume an annualized investment return of 8 percent over the term of the trust. As a result, at the end of the trust's term, the remainder value would be $745,465. This means your heirs would receive $745,000 or so without any estate or gift tax consequences.

To summarize, to the extent that your assets outperform the assumed federal AFR, you will be able to transfer that differential estate and gift tax-free. Even though you do not generally achieve meaningful income tax deductions with charitable lead trusts, you can achieve significant wealth transfer benefits by transferring the right assets in the right economic environment.

Year	Beginning Balance	Performance Growth (8%)	Annuity Payment	Ending Balance
1	$2,000,000	$160,000	$(246,600)	$1,913,400
2	1,913,400	153,072	(246,600)	1,819,872
3	1,819,872	145,590	(246,600)	1,718,862
4	1,718,862	137,509	(246,600)	1,609,771
5	1,609,771	128,782	(246,600)	1,491,953
6	1,491,953	119,356	(246,600)	1,364,709
7	1,364,709	109,177	(246,600)	1,227,286
8	1,227,286	98,183	(246,600)	1,078,869
9	1,078,869	86,310	(246,600)	918,579
10	918,579	73,486	(246,600)	745,465

Charitable Family Limited Partnerships

When discussing the split-interest charitable remainder and lead trusts, we learned that they not only provide a meaningful gift to charity, but can yield significant income tax and wealth transfer benefits to the donor, as well. There is yet another elegant technique that accomplishes all of this – the charitable family limited partnership. It is also an especially attractive technique for handling a low-basis stock concentration and where that concentration is a significant part of a family's overall wealth. Here is how it works:

1. First, you establish a family limited partnership and fund it with your stock.

2. You and your spouse become the general partners of the partnership and generally retain a small (1 percent to 2 percent) ownership interest for this position. You also own the remainder of the partnership through limited partnership interests. However, as general partner, you control the partnership, determining when to buy and sell assets and when to make distributions.

3. You then give or sell a small number of limited partnership interests to your children, either outright or through a trust. The number of

units should be such that their percentage ownership is proportionately greater than your general partnership interest. We will show you the benefits of this later.

4. You contribute the remaining limited partnership units to a charity. For this contribution, you receive a current income tax deduction equivalent to the fair market value of the property transferred, less an appropriate valuation discount for the lack of control and marketability. At the same time, you provide the charity with a "put right," which gives them the ability to sell their units back to the partnership within a given period of time. This way, the charity does not need to wait until the partnership dissolves to receive all of its funds. However, the charity would "put" its units to the partnership at fair market value, less an appropriate valuation discount.

5. It is critically important that there is no requirement for the charity to resell its units back to the partnership; otherwise, there would not be an effective gift to it in the first place. If the charity wishes to hold its units beyond the stated put-right period, it should be allowed to.

6. At some point after the gift, you, the general partner, sell the stock inside the partnership. The partnership now has cash to reinvest. This transaction will result in capital gains taxes for your general partner's share and your children's limited partners' share. However, the charity's share will realize no tax consequence, as it enjoys non-profit status.

7. At some future date, the charity decides to exercise its put right and liquidate its investment. Again, this transaction will reflect a valuation discount. When it is completed, the partnership's assets will include the value of the general partner units, the value of the children's limited partner units, and the value of the discount on the repurchase of the charity's limited partner units. As you can see, it is important for the investments in the partnership to perform well. The better the performance of the overall portfolio, the higher will be that "discount" value. Moreover, the ownership of that discount will reflect the proportionate ownership of the remaining partners – you and your children. The children's ownership of the discount effectively passes to them free of estate and gift taxes. We took care of the gift tax when the original limited partnership units were transferred to them.

8. The partnership can continue to run for many years with any appreciation on the children's units being free of wealth transfer taxation.

Perhaps the best way to clearly visualize the transaction is to look at a live example. Figure 7 illustrates this with numbers.

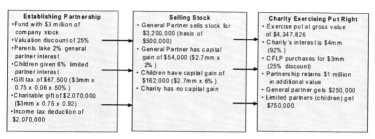

Figure 7
Charitable Family Limited Partnership (CFLP)
(An Illustration)

Establishing Partnership	Selling Stock	Charity Exercising Put Right
•Fund with $3 million of company stock	• General Partner sells stock for $3,200,000 (basis of $500,000)	• Exercise put at gross value of $4,347,826
•Valuation discount of 25%	• General Partner has capital gain of $54,000 ($2.7mm x 2%)	• Charity's interest is $4mm (92%)
•Parents take 2% general partner interest	• Children have capital gain of $162,000 ($2.7mm x 6%)	• CFLP purchases for $3mm (25% discount)
•Children given 6% limited partner interest	• Charity has no capital gain	• Partnership retains $1 million in additional value
•Gift tax of $67,500 ($3mm x 0.75 x 0.06 x 50%)		• General partner gets $250,000
•Charitable gift of $2,070,000 ($3mm x 0.75 x 0.92)		• Limited partners (children) get $750,000.
•Income tax deduction of $2,070,000		

The benefits of this technique are quite apparent. You, the donor, get a significant income tax deduction, even though it is on discounted proceeds. Your children can receive substantial assets free of gift taxes if the investment results are good. Your stock is predominately sold within the charity's account, so no capital gains are realized on most of the asset. The charity receives a significant benefit in that they do not have to wait many years to monetize a gift, as they would with a charitable remainder trust. You have greater control over investments and distributions than you do with charitable trusts. With investments, you make the decisions and do not need to worry about mandated annual distributions.

As with anything else, there are also drawbacks or risks. First, this technique is not yet ingrained in the IRS Code, so the IRS is likely to review this very thoroughly and could curb some of the benefits. Of particular interest to the IRS could be the ability to sell the stock inside the charity, thus escaping capital gains tax on most of the asset. You also have the risk that a charity may not elect to monetize and exercise its put right. If that happens, you will not realize the discount to pass along to your heirs.

Integrating Charitable and Retirement Plans

Without a doubt, the most onerous tax occurs on the transfer of qualified retirement assets. This can be an especially acute problem for corporate executives, who are likely to have significant assets in retirement vehicles. These assets get hit with both income taxes and estate and gift taxes. The reason is that qualified plans, including IRAs and 401(k) plans, are funded with pre-tax dollars that were never subject to taxation. Accordingly, if you transfer these assets to anyone other than your spouse during your lifetime, the income tax needs to be paid first. Even if you contribute retirement assets to a charity in your lifetime, you could very well incur adverse income tax consequences, as you first need to take the distribution, pay the income tax, and then contribute to charity. While you may get a charitable deduction, you could run into gross income limitations in a given year, as we will discuss in the next chapter.

As a result, retirement transfers usually take place at death. Here again, the tax situation is cumbersome. Let's back up for a moment and consider the concept behind the potential double taxation of retirement plans at death.

The concept revolves around the rule of "income in respect of decedent" (IRD). This is a probate term that relates to income the decedent earned during his or her lifetime but did not yet report on a tax return, or income that was never taxed. The retirement funds fall into the category of never being taxed. So the retirement funds become income on your final income tax return. At the same time, the transfer of your retirement assets to anyone other than your spouse will result in estate tax. You are not double-taxed completely, however, as you receive a deduction on the income tax return for estate taxes paid. Let's look at an example:

Assume you have an estate of $5 million, with $2 million in qualified retirement assets.

- The estate tax on the retirement funds would be $1 million.

- Before calculating the final income tax, you would take a $1 million deduction from the $2 million retirement value and then apply the tax. Assuming the marginal rate of 39 percent, the income tax would be $390,000.

- The total tax on the retirement funds would be $1,390,000 or nearly 70 percent of its value.

Something obviously needs to be done to mitigate this crippling taxation. Charitable options can largely accomplish that. We will briefly mention some of these techniques, indicating advantages and drawbacks of each:

1. You can provide a testamentary gift directly to a charity. This enables you to escape both the income tax and the estate tax. While you gain no tax benefits against other income, you do alleviate

paying huge taxes. The drawback is that your spouse could be left with inadequate funds.

2. Alternatively, you could name your spouse as the primary beneficiary of your plan, with the charity as the secondary, or contingent, beneficiary. This accomplishes the same thing from a tax standpoint, as your spouse can roll over your IRA or other plans into hers.

3. You could again use the charitable remainder trust as part of the solution. One option is to establish the charitable remainder trust as the primary beneficiary, with your spouse as the lifetime annuitant. At your spouse's death, the remainder assets go to charity. This escapes both the income tax and the estate tax again. One disadvantage is that your spouse is limited to the CRT annual payment and does not have some of the flexibilities contained in some traditional trusts. This could be a problem with top-heavy retirement estates.

4. Another option is to name your spouse the primary beneficiary and a charitable remainder trust as the secondary beneficiary. Your children could be the annuitants under the CRT. However, if anyone other than a spouse ultimately receives the funds, there will be tax implications. With a CRT, the children would pay income taxes on the distributions they receive. There will also be estate tax implications on the present value of their payments, calculated at the second spouse's death.

5. Still another alternative is to place some of your retirement assets into a charitable remainder unitrust and then have that unitrust become part of an overall credit shelter trust. The credit shelter trust is a trust equal to your estate tax exemption amount. This enables you to stretch your retirement assets beyond your spouse, as monies in a credit shelter trust can go to the next generation.

Retirement planning and charitable gifts have another dimension in that certain charitable vehicles can be retirement funds in and of themselves. For example, you could contribute a low-dividend stock to a charity in return for a charitable gift annuity. This augmented income can serve you during retirement. Another example centers on a younger person who establishes a deferred gift annuity. Here the payments do not begin until some time in the future. You have the ability to build capital if your stock or other assets appreciate over the years, and you potentially have an augmented income stream when you retire. Charitable remainder trust variations such as NICRUTs and NIMCRUTs, as we discussed earlier, can also serve as effective enhancements to your retirement picture.

Generation-skipping Transfers and CLUTs

Another important tax concept centers on the tax on transfers to individuals who are two or more generations below you – your grandchildren. In addition to estate tax, you are also subject to a generation-skipping transfer tax on such gifts. This tax is at the same general level as the estate tax. However, each person gets a lifetime exemption from this tax up to approximately $1 million.

Generation-skipping transfers offer some interesting planning opportunities when done within charitable lead unitrusts (CLUTs). To reiterate, the CLUT provides for an annual payment to charity for a specified number of years. At termination, the remainder interest passes back to you, your spouse, or your heirs. To the extent it passes to someone other than your spouse, there is a taxable gift. Furthermore, if it passes to grandchildren, it would also be subject to generation-skipping tax. There is a neat transaction that allows you to combine the CLUT with a family dynasty trust and sell the remainder interest of the CLUT to the dynasty trust. Figure 8 illustrates such a transaction, and following are the steps involved.

Figure 8
Sale of Remainder Interest in CLAT (or GRUT) to Dynasty Trust

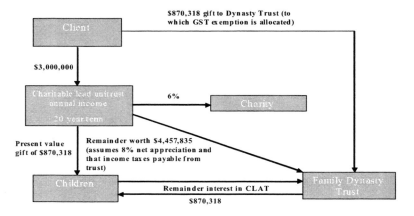

1. You first establish a $3,000,000 CLUT by contributing your company stock, along with any other assets. The term of the trust is 20 years, with the remainder interest going to your children. The annual payout to the charity is set at 6 percent, payable at the end of each year. The applicable federal APR is 4 percent. Using the annuity tables, this translates into an $870,318 remainder interest or present value gift to your children.

2. You and your spouse set up a family dynasty trust, which is a grantor trust for income tax purposes. This means you are taxed on the income.

3. You and your spouse transfer at least an additional $870,318 of assets into this family trust. Upon doing so, you allocate part of your generation-skipping transfer tax exemption. On the other hand, this transfer is not a gift because you are actually transferring it to yourself, as the grantor of the trust.

4. The family trust then purchases the remainder interest of the CLUT from the children at today's present value, which is the $870,318. It is possible that there will be some income tax liability for the children, based on the gain embedded in their remainder interest. However, this is a true sale without any gift tax consequences.

5. At the end of 20 years, any appreciation within the CLUT passes to future generations via the family trust, without GST consequences. If we assume long-term net appreciation (after taxes) of 8 percent, we would expect the remainder to be worth $4,457,835 in 20 years. Again, this money would pass to future generations free of estate taxes, as well as generation-skipping transfer taxes.

As a final note on this technique, you could set the initial remainder interest even lower by increasing the charitable unitrust percentage or increasing the term. In fact, it could be set to zero, as shown earlier. The lower it is, the less paid by the family trust for the remainder interest, and the less income tax liability the children have on the sale. On the other hand, the charity will get more funds, and you risk having considerably less in the CLUT at termination, particularly if the investment results fall short of expectations.

Gifting ESOP Replacement Assets to a CRT

One of the exit strategies for the owners of a privately held company is to create an Employee Stock Ownership Plan (ESOP) and sell their stock to the plan. The tax code permits the owners to defer capital gain recognition if the proceeds are invested in what is termed "qualified replacement property." This property generally includes securities issued by domestic corporations with secondary market trading available. The resulting portfolio is commonly called a 1042 rollover portfolio, named after the IRS code section governing this type of transaction. The replacement assets carry the owner's original cost basis, so capital gains taxes would be due when any of the replacement assets are sold. A buy-and-hold strategy is fine, so long as your investment objective does not change. However, if you wish to rearrange the assets to generate more income at retirement, you would be stuck unless you wanted to incur capital gains taxes.

There is a way out of this if you are willing to contribute the assets to a charitable remainder trust. By doing this, the trust can later sell the securities and reposition the portfolio to meet your needs. Moreover, if you establish one of the CRT variations, such as a NIMCRUT, you can create additional retirement planning flexibility.

Increasing Annuity Charitable Lead Annuity Trust

We will conclude this chapter with two less complicated techniques. The first is to establish a standard CLAT, but to increase the fixed annual charitable payout each year. When setting up the CLAT, you might structure it to be a zeroed-out CLAT based on its first-year annuity payout rate. Assuming a reasonable investment return, you then have the flexibility to increase the payout annually, perhaps by 20 percent.

The benefit of structuring the CLAT this way is to enable funds to remain in the trust for a longer period of time. While the charity will ultimately get all of the monies you intended it to receive, your heirs may end up getting more by having these additional funds invested for a longer time period.

QTIP Remainder Trust

Finally, you can structure your estate to involve a qualified terminable interest trust wherein you provide for your spouse while he or she is still alive. This trust qualifies for the unlimited marital deduction. Then, at the death of the surviving spouse, you direct the assets to go to a charity.

Your spouse's estate would receive a charitable deduction for the monies passing to charity. Some people may prefer a simpler approach like this to a more formalized charitable remainder trust. While this approach provides no current income tax benefits, it does give the spouse added flexibility with the funds as you can provide for some limited principal invasion.

There are many different alternatives as there are ways to combine the various techniques. As we will discuss later, no single strategy may fit all of your objectives. It may be necessary to adopt several different ones over time.

SIX

WHAT ASSETS?
HOW MUCH TO CONTRIBUTE

You decided which structures to use and probably also decided which
You decided which structures to use and probably also decided which
assets to contribute. However, you still need to determine how much to
contribute after figuring out the true tax benefits of your planned
approach. The tax code offers varying incentives based on several key
factors. What may surprise you is that there are limits as to how much
you can actually contribute in any given tax year and still receive tax
benefits. After reviewing these charitable deduction limits, we will
consider some of the major asset types you can and might contribute to
philanthropic structures.

The General Rules

Before you start, there are some general, overall rules governing
contributions of property:

- First, the recipient must be a qualified charitable organization as
  delineated in the IRS code.

- You must contribute cash, marketable securities, or other qualified
  property, as permitted by the IRS.

- Your charitable income tax deduction is limited to a specific
  percentage of your adjusted gross income as reported on your tax
  return.

- You do have a tax carry-forward allowance for any unused
  deduction. The carry-forward is generally for five years.

Charitable Deduction Limits

Policy makers considered the following factors when categorizing the various limitations for tax purposes:

- Whether the contribution is to a public or private foundation.

- Whether you are contributing cash or other property.

- Whether the gifted property is considered ordinary income and short-term capital gain *versus* long-term capital gain property. To derive the status of any property, you consider whether its immediate sale would generate a short- or long-term capital gain today.

The chart below summarizes the major charitable deduction limitations:

	Public Charities/ Community Foundations	Private Foundations
Cash	**50% of AGI***	**30% of AGI***
Ordinary income and short-term capital gain property	50% of AGI	30% of AGI
Valuation method	Cost	Cost
Long-term capital gain property	30% of AGI	20% of AGI
Valuation method	Fair Market Value	Cost (but marketable securities at Fair Market Value)
Tangible property	50% of AGI	30% of AGI
Valuation method	Cost	Cost

*Adjusted gross income

Here's how these limitations may apply to you:

1. Gifts to public charities carry the most favorable limitations. These entities include the traditional institutions, such as universities and hospitals. They also cover community foundations, most supporting organizations, and donor advised funds. You can transfer cash and ordinary income assets to these entities up to 50 percent of your adjusted gross income in any taxable year with a five-year carry-forward for any unused deduction. If you are transferring appreciated securities, you are limited to 30 percent of your AGI, but the contribution amount would be the fair market value of the asset.

When you contribute most tangible property, you can do so at a 50 percent rate, but its valuation is at cost.

2. With gifts to private foundations, you experience lower AGI limits at all levels. For cash and ordinary income property, you are limited to 30 percent of your AGI. For appreciated securities, your limit is 20 percent, but again, the valuation is fair market value. For private foundations, only marketable securities can be valued at fair market value. Others are valued at cost.

3. For charitable remainder trusts, the limitations will depend on who gets the remainder interest. For example, if the remainder interests are restricted to public charities, the public charity column will apply. On the other hand, should a private foundation be designated as the remainder organization, the AGI limitations would be the same as the private foundation column.

4. Charitable lead trusts are treated differently. First, non-grantor charitable lead trusts have no income tax implications. If the trust is a grantor charitable lead trust, and the lead interest goes to a public charity, the tax deduction is limited to a 30 percent ceiling on cash and ordinary income property and 20 percent on capital gain property with a five-year carry-forward. If the lead interest is to a private foundation, a 20 percent ceiling is imposed, with no five-year carry-forward benefit.

5. These charitable AGI limitations do not pyramid over each other. More specifically, all gifts are subject to the highest, or 50 percent, overall limitation. Lower-level gifts at 30 percent or 20 percent will be reduced by the amount contributed at the 50 percent level.

Let's look at a quick example, where your AGI is $300,000 this year, and you wish to contribute $100,000 of company stock directly to your alma mater. You also have a private foundation and would like to provide additional funding for that. From a tax perspective, you will be able to contribute only an additional $50,000 of assets to gain tax benefits, since your limitation is $150,000. If you did not give the stock to your alma mater, you could transfer 30 percent of your AGI, or $90,000, to your private foundation.

Review of Major Gift Assets

The tax laws cover a wide range of assets that can be contributed to charity. However, taxes alone will not always govern whether a particular asset contribution will work. You can contribute certain assets to one charitable structure but not to another, as we will see. Moreover, some charities will not accept certain assets that are difficult to manage or sell. To stay within our general purpose, we will not cover every asset category, nor will we cover any one asset in tremendous depth. Some of the rules surrounding certain assets are complicated, so you should consult your tax counsel if you have unique assets you may wish to contribute to charity.

Here is a review of some of the major asset types:

Cash

While cash provides you with the maximum 50 percent deduction, you should probably not use it if you have appreciated securities you are willing to contribute. However, if cash is your dominant asset because of the exercise of stock options or the sale of your company, you would obviously want to give the cash to gain an immediate income tax deduction.

Publicly Traded Securities

Without question, this is the most popular gift from the perspectives of both the donor and the charity. For the donor, these gifts provide a fair market value deduction, are simple to transfer, and are readily priced by the market. Charities like these gifts because they can be liquidated easily. Publicly traded securities encompass a wide range of assets, although the common forms are stocks, bonds, and mutual funds. On the other hand, there are a few nuances about some forms of securities that you should check out before deciding to contribute them to a charity.

- *Restricted stock transfers* can be tricky. More specifically, if you transfer restricted stock to a charitable trust, the restriction remains, since you still have a partial interest in these trusts. However, if you make a direct contribution to a charity and hold the stock for at least two years, you are probably "safe," as long as the charity does not own more than 10 percent of the shares and is not considered an affiliate.

- *Contributing options and futures* is also tricky, as you need to properly allocate gains and losses between long- and short-term.

- With *real estate investment trusts and master limited partnerships,* you need to be aware of unrelated business taxable income.

Closely Held Business Interests

Contributing C Corporation shares to a charitable remainder trust can be very advantageous if the company appreciates and is ultimately sold. The gain will escape immediate taxation and will not be realized until you receive distributions. On the other hand, you need to be careful that none of the private foundation rules (such as unrelated business income tax, jeopardy investments, excess business holdings, and self-dealing) are violated.

Consider the situation wherein you contribute your closely held stock to a charitable remainder trust. Assume you and your family own more than 35 percent of the company before contributing. If the company later offers to redeem those shares, your trust could be violating the self-dealing rules, unless the company goes through an elaborate procedure of offering to redeem shares of all stockholders.

If you recall, you can eliminate these private foundation limitations if you are contributing your stock to a supporting organization. If you are contributing S-corporation stock, you need to be aware of the same foundation rules, along with other key issues. First, you cannot contribute S-corporation shares to a charitable remainder trust. Such transfers are not tax deductible; the trust would lose its tax exemption for that year (as it would have unrelated business income), and it is possible the company could even lose its S-corporation status.

On the other hand, you can contribute these investments to a grantor charitable lead trust, since all income is taxed directly to you. If you contribute S-corporation shares to your private foundation, your tax deduction is based on your cost and not market value. Finally, the gift of S-corporation shares is not always great for the charity, as all income is considered unrelated business income and therefore subject to taxation. It is critically important to consult both your personal and your corporate counsel before contemplating gifts of business interests.

Real Estate

This asset type also has its operating complexities, and many charities have specific terms for accepting real estate assets. Charities are generally concerned with complete title to the property, debt on the property, poor marketability, rental vacancies, and environmental deficiencies. On the other hand, clean real estate offers some excellent planning opportunities for donors. Here are some of them:

1. You can fund a deferred gift annuity with real estate. Since you do not begin receiving your annuity until some time in the future, you can let the property remain in the gift until you get closer to the time when the payments begin. This gives the charity time to prepare for the sale. Many charities do not readily take real estate in current gift annuities, unless the property can be sold rather quickly.

2. Funding a charitable remainder trust with real estate is another option, but be careful if it has a mortgage (UBIT issues). Of particular interest are the two variations – the NICRUT and the NIMCRUT – since the trust pays you only the lesser of the earned income or the unitrust percentage. The NIMCRUT allows for a make-up later. These transactions allow you to enhance your annual cash flow when the property is later sold. Also, you get an immediate income tax benefit when contributing the asset.

3. Perhaps the best set-up is to use a Flip Unitrust to handle real estate. This structure starts out as a regular NICRUT where you are paid the lesser of the earned income or the unitrust amount. The trust flips to a unitrust at a future date or event that you may specify. For instance, you can specify that the flip takes place when the property is sold.

Conservation Easements

If you have property that has conservation, historic, or scenic value, you can pursue favorable tax treatment for contributing it to a qualified organization. Assuming you are successful in donating the property, you can realize income, estate, and property tax benefits. Your charitable income tax deduction is based on the value before and after contribution. Moreover, you can sometimes start with an appraisal that takes into account the highest and best use, which would include any development rights. Estate tax deductions also account for the imputed value contributed with additional amounts for certain types of property. Finally, property taxes are likewise reduced.

Life Insurance

Life insurance affects charitable structures in a variety of ways, and it is certainly beyond our scope to cover this topic in great detail. A few aspects of insurance and their impact on charitable planning are nevertheless worth mentioning, even if our discussion is incomplete.

First, life insurance is a valuable asset in making the charitable remainder trust work in certain situations. As you recall, insurance is used as a wealth replacement tool to provide heirs with assets to cover the remainder funds going to charity. Furthermore, deferred annuities can be the funding vehicle for NIMCRUTs, which will enable funds to grow on a tax-deferred basis until needed in the future, when you are in a lower tax bracket and in retirement. Still another option is to use insurance in combination with Flip Unitrusts. Here, you would contribute funds to the flip trust, taking an annual income tax deduction and using the funds to purchase insurance. Your death would become the "triggering" event that flips the trust to a straight percentage unitrust.

Insurance is also used to in other ways. In some instances, it is employed to guarantee charitable gift annuities. Finally, you can just give an insurance policy to a charity, but there is a set of laws governing the tax deductibility of doing so. In many instances, you are limited to the cost or replacement value.

Tangible Personal Property

There are also rules for contributing personal property. We will not discuss this in any detail, except to comment on art collections. There is a distinction between art you created and art someone else created. If you are the painter, for instance, you can deduct only the cost of producing the painting and not any appraised appreciation. On the other hand, if you purchased the painting and later contributed it, you are entitled the fair market value deduction.

Intangible Property

For the sake of completeness, you should know there are tax benefits for contributing such properties as royalties, copyrights, and patents. However, we will not cover those specifics here. Your tax and estate planning adviser will help you make your best decisions on these kinds of property.

SEVEN

DIVERSIFICATION STRATEGIES FOR LOW-BASIS STOCKS

We are now at a point where we stop and try to pull together all of the concepts in an effort to develop a coherent plan. Much of our discussion centered on ways to employ charitable techniques to diversify away low-basis concentrated equity positions. Until now, we've looked at each technique separately – in a vacuum, so to speak. We will now look at how you combine the charitable with other financial techniques to design an overall program. We will look at this from the vantage point of the corporate executive with a substantial amount of family wealth tied up in the company stock. These strategies go beyond just the executive, however, and can apply to anyone with a large concentrated stock position.

We should start by indicating the various financial techniques that complement and supplement the charitable structures already discussed. In the appendix to this chapter, we present a series of tables highlighting some, but not all, of these financial strategies. There are several other financial strategies, including some advanced ones, but our purpose here is to just establish a decision process. The specific financial strategies we include are:

- Outright sales
- Purchase of a put option
- Costless collar

- Variable share prepaid forward sale
- 1 x 2 call spread
- Exchange funds
- Grantor Retained Annuity Trust (GRAT)

To assist in this process, we've prepared two decision templates. In Figure 9, below, we first constructed a diversification template showing the various decision inputs you might consider at any point in time. We then showed the various financial and charitable strategies we might employ to achieve our objectives.

Figure 9
Concentrated Equity Strategies

Diversification Template

Decision Inputs	**Strategies**
• Downside price risk	• Sales
• Upside price potential	• Private hedging
• Diversification	• Hedging & monetization
• Tax deferral	• Exchange funds
• Income/cash flow needs	• Charitable remainder trusts
• Investment opportunities	• NICRUT/NIMCRUT
• Liquidity	• Grantor retained annuity trusts
• Market perception	• Charitable lead trusts
• Charitable interests	• Family limited partnerships
• Interest rate levels	integrated with trusts
• Restricted Securities	• 1 x 2 call spreads/GRAT
• Insider/affiliate	
• Age	

In Figure 10, on the following page, we suggested what strategies you may wish to employ based on your valuation of the stock. Now we will briefly discuss each decision input, suggesting some possible strategies to deal with each, assuming the particular input is important to you.

Before we start, bear in mind the following overall strategy considerations:

- Rarely will you want to adopt just one strategy and stay with it forever. An efficient program generally employs multiple strategies, initiated over time.

- Be flexible to changing market dynamics, such as stock price and interest rates.

- Timing is important when you pull the trigger on using any one technique.

- Unfortunately, many of these techniques are irrevocable, once established.

Figure 10
Single Stock Strategies

Insert "Table 4" (Retitled "Figure 10") in landscape layout on this page.

Strategy / Stock Valuation	Outright Sale	1 x 2 Call Spread	Put Option	Costless Collars	Var. Prpd. Forward Sale	Exchange Fund	Charitable Remainder Trusts	NICRUT/ NIMCRUT	FLP w/ Trusts
Undervalued		▓						▓	▓
Slightly undervalued		▓					▓	▓	▓
Fairly Valued	▓				▓			▓	
Slightly overvalued			▓	▓	▓	▓			
Overvalued	▓		▓	▓					

- Multiple inputs can be important to you at any time. Not every input can be critically important, though, and some conflict with each other. You may need to prioritize.

Downside Price Risk

If you are concerned about the downside and consider the stock to be overvalued, you have many options. You can certainly sell some of the stock, pay the capital gain, and move on. This is sometimes the best strategy. If you have a foundation, this may be a good time to contribute some of the stock. On the other hand, if you feel the stock is fairly valued and wish to continue holding it, you can just protect your position by doing a collar where your downside is covered and you retain some upside during the course of the contract. If the stock price exceeds the cap price at expiration, you can always settle in cash to avoid selling any part of your position. You also have the option of doing a variable prepaid forward sale if you want more upside participation and the other benefits of this transaction. Alternatively, a charitable remainder trust makes sense, particularly if you are indifferent about holding onto all of your position and you believe the stock is reasonably valued.

Upside Price Potential

When you believe the stock is undervalued with strong upside potential, it is generally a good time to consider intra-family wealth transfer planning, employing GRATs, family limited partnerships, and similar options. On the charitable side, this is a good time to put the stock into one of the charitable trust variations, such as a NICRUT or a NIMCRUT. If you have a charitable lead unitrust, this is also an opportune time to fund it or add to it with some of your stock position.

As to financial products, a 1x2 call spread strategy might be timely if you believe the upside is there but perhaps limited to 35 percent to 40 percent or so. On the other hand, if you believe there is no real upside but are also not very concerned about the downside, you might find a charitable remainder trust appropriate if the other reasons exist to establish one.

Diversification/Tax Deferral

You have decided you want to diversify out of some of your position but want to do it in a tax-deferred way. Charitable remainder trusts certainly allow you to accomplish this, assuming you want to provide the future funds to charity. A popular financial strategy is the exchange fund, which effectively defers payment of taxes. Likewise, the variable prepaid forward sale provides diversification and tax deferral.

Income/Cash Flow Needs

Your stock carries a low dividend, and you are trying to position your portfolio for retirement, when you will require a greater cash flow from your investments. As we discussed earlier, charitable remainder trusts accomplish this very well. The offshoots, NICRUTs and NIMCRUTs, are even more potent as tools to enhance income from a low-dividend stock.

Investment Opportunities

A common need, particularly among executives who want to stay active in the business world, is to find ways to monetize their concentrated stock holdings to fund new ventures. While you can always go to your banker and borrow the money against your stock position, a more elegant solution is to engage in a variable prepaid forward sale. You get your money (although discounted for the embedded interest cost), just as with a loan, but you also protect any downside price risk on the stock while deferring taxes. Also, if you are going to reinvest the proceeds in margin stocks, a bank loan is restricted by Regulation U to 50 percent of the pledged stock value.

Liquidity

Again, the variable prepaid forward sales will provide immediate liquidity for investment or other purposes. Obviously, an outright sale accomplishes that, as well, provided you are willing to pay taxes. If, on the other hand, you just want a stronger cash flow with more favorable tax consequences, the charitable remainder trust may work again.

Market Perception

When you hold a concentrated position in a company and you are also an insider, you are sometimes concerned about how the market will view your sale and diversification transactions. Outright sales are sometimes viewed differently from collars and forward sales, and charitable remainder trusts are viewed differently from each of them. With a charitable trust, the stock is not considered a sale until sold within the trust. Finally, wealth transfers within the family generally escape notice.

Charitable Interests

Many financial counselors will tell you taxes are not generally the sole driving force for individuals to establish charitable structures. The charitable desire and intent must be there.

Interest Rate Levels

Low interest rates present tremendous wealth transfer opportunities through two of the techniques. The concept behind this lies in the way split-interest trusts are valued by the IRS. As discussed earlier, a charitable lead trust is expected to grow at the federal discount rate (APR), and this is the rate at which the remainder interest is valued for gift tax purposes. To the extent that the actual growth rate exceeds the expected rate, that difference will pass to your heirs free of estate and gift taxes. On the non-charitable side, the grantor retained annuity trust will provide a similar benefit to your heirs, as they receive the remainder interest, while you receive the annual annuity.

Restricted Securities and Insider/Affiliate Status

A host of laws govern restricted securities and the trading activities of corporate insiders and affiliates. Again, a full discussion of this topic is beyond our scope, but it is important to note that all of the structures and strategies are subject to these rules. Consulting with both your personal tax adviser and corporate counsel is imperative before you consider any of these strategies if you have restricted shares or are an insider.

Age

Finally, your age may also govern what strategies are best to employ at any particular time. Conversely, age can also govern what strategies may not be effective. For example, charitable remainder trusts may not work for certain combinations of age and payout rate, particularly for younger individuals. Also, lifetime CRT annuities will not provide a great tax deduction, so you may be better with a stated term if you are younger than 55.

On the other hand, if you are younger, a NIMCRUT can be attractive, since you are not drawing out considerable funds in the beginning years.

No One Strategy ...

The above decision inputs can't be considered as isolated factors. In reality, you will experience multiple issues at any one time. For instance, you could be in a situation in which you have a good investment opportunity, believe the stock has good upside, and interest rates are low. No one strategy will capture all of what you wish to accomplish, so you may need to either prioritize or embark on more than one strategy at a time.

Chapter 7 Appendix
Financial Liquidity Strategies

Alternatives	Description	Advantages	Disadvantages
Outright Stock Sale (Insiders may adopt a 10b51plan to get through blackout periods)	• Open market transaction. • Market or spot secondary offering. • Block sales	• Receive immediate liquidity. • Benefit of marketing effort by investment banker. • Easy to execute. • Protected against price declines.	• Taxable sale. • May impact market and subject to discounts. • No future price appreciation in shares sold.
Purchase of a Protective Put Option	• Gives purchaser the right to sell the underlying stock at a predetermined price at some future date • Generally able to purchase puts up to 5 times daily trading volume.	• Full downside protection on stock below put strike price. • Ownership, dividends, and voting rights maintained. • Investor retains full upside potential. • Cash settlement of option can defer sale of position.	• Out-of-pocket cost for option
Costless Collar	• Purchase of a put option with a strike price at or below current price, combined with sale of a call option with a strike price above current price • Both have same maturity. • Premium from sale of call offsets purchase price of put. • Can collar up to 5 times daily volume. • Maturities range from 1 to 5 years.	• Full downside protection below put strike price. • Upside participation to the call strike price. • Retain voting rights and dividends. • Cash settlement defers sale of position. • No out-of-pocket expense.	• No upside beyond call strike price. • Exposure to downside from current to put strike price. • No liquidity generated unless a loan is obtained.

Alternatives	Description	Advantages	Disadvantages
Variable	• Investor sells stock	• Defer taxable sale.	• Limited participation

Share Prepaid Forward Sale (VPF)	forward, subject to a variable share delivery formula. • Counterparty sets floor and cap prices. • Investor receives upfront proceeds based on discount to floor price. • Investor delivers stock at maturity based on final price at expiration. • Maturities range from 1 to 5 years. • A variation of the VPF is a Participating VPF: Investor retains full upside potential on a limited number of shares, but receives smaller upfront proceeds compared to standard VPF transaction.	• Hedge downside exposure while retaining upside appreciation up to the cap price. On a Participating VPF, upside participation is full on a position of the shares. • Ability to monetize well over 50%, and investor faces no reinvestment restrictions. • Retain voting rights and dividends. • Cash settlement can further defer sale of position.	above cap price. • Imbedded financing cost. • Investor exposed down to floor price. • Dividend increases paid to counterparty. • Tax complexity.
1 x 2 Call Spread	• Involves the purchase of an in-the-money call option and the sale of two out-of-the-money call options. The premiums offset each other. • You are able to increase appreciation potential within a specified range with no out-of-pocket expenses.	• Leverages return within a predetermined price range. • You continue to enjoy ownership and voting rights. • You retain dividends and can settle in cash, as opposed to selling the position.	• If stock price soars above the price of the sold call options, you do not share in the appreciation. • No additional downside protection. • Not all stocks will qualify if the counterparty cannot borrow the stock and maintain a short position.
Exchange Funds	• A limited partnership where participants contribute highly appreciated stock for	• Immediate diversification. • Tax deferral.	• Investment performance risk. • Illiquidity, as many will run 7 years.

a share of ownership.
- Each fund has a predetermined termination date.
- At least 20% of the fund to be in qualified, less liquid investments, such as preferred operating units of real estate operating partnerships (affiliated with publicly traded REITs). Funds may borrow to purchase these investments or require some cash contributions from participants.

- At end of term, distributions can be in original stock or basket of portfolio stocks. No tax event until securities are sold.
- Attractive estate planning tool because of valuation discounts and estate freeze options.

- Tax liability on early redemption.
- No control over portfolio management process.

Grantor Retained Annuity Trust (GRAT)

- Grantor (investor) establishes an irrevocable trust and contributes assets to it.
- Grantor receives an annuity for the term of the trust.
- The remainder passes to another individual, usually children.
- The present value of the remainder interest is a taxable gift.
- Appreciation over the taxable gift amount passes to the remainder beneficiary.
- If grantor dies before term expires, assets brought back to his or her estate.

- Attractive in low interest rate environment, particularly if assets grow at a rate in excess of the federal AFR.
- Can be funded with restricted stock.
- Can be paid back with in-kind assets.
- Grantor pays tax on income earned within GRAT.

- Must outlive the term of the GRAT or assets flow back to estate.
- If performance is less than the federal AFR, you paid gift taxes for nothing, unless it was a zeroed-out GRAT.

EIGHT

INVESTMENT MANAGEMENT

Ask any investment advisers about their view of the financial markets. Almost certainly, among their first ten words will be the word "volatility." Many professional investors accept market turbulence, emphasizing that their clients are in the market for the long haul. Generally, this is a very appropriate reaction to short-term market volatility. With charitable structures, short-term volatility is also acceptable – provided it remains short-term. Successive years of downside volatility create operating problems, even if the long-term investment program works out. Many charitable structures depend on achieving a minimum rate of return to meet their charitable commitments, particularly when multi-year gifts are involved. Therefore, managing charitable funds involves more than just achieving market or peer-group benchmarks. You or your fiduciary advisers also need to structure portfolios to mitigate severe downside risk, realizing that total risk elimination can be achieved only by holding treasury bills.

This chapter is devoted to the process of designing, implementing, and monitoring investment policies and strategies for charitable portfolios. Common investment themes transcend all portfolios, whether they are individual, charitable, corporate, pension, or endowment. Also within the charitable field are some common principles of portfolio construction. At the same time, each charitable structure has its own nuances that we must take into account when designing investment portfolios. To that end, our approach is to look at the major charitable entities separately, suggesting an investment approach that is consistent with each one's financial objectives and unique operating structure. We will devote considerable space to developing investment strategies for private family foundations.

LIFETIME GIFTS

There are three general types of lifetime gifts:

With *charitable gift annuities,* you really have no investment decisions, since you rely on the credit of the charity to fulfill its annual annuity obligation to you. You can sometimes have the charity purchase an insurance policy backing up that credit, but the cost of the policy reduces your annual payment.

You can fund *deferred gift annuities* with real estate, as we mentioned in the previous chapter, and have the charity hold that asset until a future date closer to the time when the annuity payments begin. On the other hand, if you contribute cash or securities, the charity will invest the funds itself, giving you a promise to pay, based on their financial standing.

With *pooled income funds,* you actually do have some investment discretion, as charities usually have funds to which you can direct your money. The fund or funds you select will determine your annual payout, as you are paid on the income earned within each fund. Generally, there are fund offerings along these lines:

1. Beginning with conservative investments, there could be a *capital preservation fund* that invests in money market and perhaps short-term government investments.

2. There is always an *income fund* that invests in government, mortgaged-backed, and corporate bonds of varying maturities. Some of these funds may also include high dividend-paying stocks in the portfolio. The objective is optimal current income. Older individuals may find this option attractive.

3. You can also expect that there will be a *balanced fund* that consists of an equal weighting of equities and fixed income.

4. Moving along the risk curve, you are likely to find a *growth fund* consisting of a higher weighting of equity securities, but with some remaining exposure (20 percent to 30 percent) to bonds. While your income will be considerably lower with this selection, you are hopeful that the portfolio will grow, and as it does, your annual income will grow with it.

5. Finally, there may be an *aggressive growth* alternative that is an all-equity portfolio. This could be appropriate for a younger individual who wishes to build a future income stream from an increasing asset base.

CRATs and CRUTs: Common Guidelines

Here is where you begin to exert some meaningful investment discretion. At the same time, you or the trustee will be accountable to adhere to federal tax regulations and fiduciary standards of investing. We will consider the charitable remainder annuity trust (CRAT) and the charitable remainder unitrust (CRUT) separately, but there are a couple of common investment rules and guidelines that pertain to both, and we will consider those first:

Four-tier Tax System

We discussed earlier that a key advantage of charitable remainder trusts is the ability to sell appreciated securities within the trust but defer paying the capital gains taxes until the funds are distributed to you over time. The "time" has now arrived, and we will go over how the taxes work on CRT distributions. As the CRT is a tax-exempt entity, taxes are paid by the lifetime annuitant with annual distributions categorized within a four-tier system. The order of taxation is as follows:

1. *Ordinary income:* To the extent that the CRT has ordinary taxable interest and dividends in a given year, these amounts are considered to be distributed first. There is also a carryover situation in that any prior year's undistributed ordinary income is considered to be distributed next before moving to the next distribution tier.

2. *Capital gains:* The next level of distributions entails capital gains. Following the same pattern, to the extent that the trust first has short-term capital gains in the current year, as well as undistributed short-term gains from the prior year, it is considered to be distributed next. Long-term capital gains are considered next in the same fashion.

3. *Tax-exempt income:* Once your distribution absorbs the ordinary income and the capital gains components, the next to be distributed is any tax-free income, both for the current year and for any prior year's undistributed tax-free income.

4. *Return of capital:* Finally, to the extent that you have any remaining distributable income in a given year, it will be considered a return of your original capital.

An example might better illustrate how this distribution pattern works:

- Assume your CRAT has an annual distribution of $60,000.

- This year, the trust earned $10,000 in ordinary interest and dividends, along with $20,000 of municipal bond interest. The trustee also sold some of your contributed company stock this year for a long-term capital gain of $15,000. Last year, the trustee sold stock, too, but had a carryover gain of $12,000.

- The current year's distribution would be classified as follows for tax purposes: $10,000 is classified as ordinary taxable income; $15,000 from this year and $12,000 from last year are considered long-term capital gains; $20,000 is classified as municipal bond income; and $3,000 is considered a return of capital.

This tax rule has a couple of implications for your investment strategy. First, you will want to allocate your fixed-income assets to municipal bonds, as opposed to taxable bonds unless, of course, the yield spreads dictate otherwise. As for your concentrated low-basis stock (assuming you contributed this type of asset to the trust), you need to keep in mind that all of the gains your trustee incurs by selling the appreciated stock will need to be distributed before any of your municipal bond income. Therefore, you may wish to time the sales of your stock if it is not inconsistent with the timing of your investment objective to diversify.

Unrelated Business Income Tax

An important regulatory restriction centers on the issue of unrelated business income. Many years ago, charitable non-profit organizations became engaged in running for-profit businesses. This obviously gave the charity an unfair advantage over its commercial competitors, since it enjoyed tax-exempt status. Consequently, charitable organizations, for many years now, have been restricted from using their tax-free status to achieve an unfair competitive commercial advantage.

Simply defined, unrelated business income is any income earned from a trade or business that is not substantially related to the mission or purpose of the charitable entity. The definition also reaches to include debt-financed income from such activities as real estate, margined securities, and certain hedge funds. The actual tax penalties vary by charitable entity. Consider these examples:

- For private foundations and supporting organizations, unrelated business income results in regular taxable income with the risk of losing its tax-exempt status if it has too much unrelated business income.

- Charitable remainder trusts are the most penalized, as they will be taxed not only on the unrelated business income in any given year, but on all of their income.

- Charitable lead trusts are not hit as hard. Non-grantor CLTs will pay a partial tax, and grantor CLTs will not incur any tax ramifications, since the grantor pays the taxes on the trust's income.

Charitable Remainder Annuity Trusts

This entity, as you recall, features a fixed-dollar annuity that is set upon inception of the portfolio. This carries both opportunity and risk. If you outperform the federal APR that was used to calculate the charitable remainder interest, you will benefit the charity. If you underperform, you hurt the charity. With the CRAT, one could argue that the risk of poor performance is more important than any lost marginal opportunity to outperform on the upside. Significant underperformance could also jeopardize having any funds left over for the charity or for meeting your annuity payments in later years. Investment results are generally a function of asset allocation and the performance of the securities within each asset class. The securities can be managed individually, through mutual funds or through partnerships. For the purpose of looking at investment strategies for charitable trusts, we will focus only on asset allocation. We will save our discussion on manager or mutual fund selection for our coverage of foundation investment management in Chapter 9.

Generally, a CRAT should feature some balance between equities and bonds. Even though you must meet a fixed-dollar payment, you may be best positioned to accomplish that with an increasing asset base and just sell positions to meet the annuity payments. On the other hand, you would also want to take advantage of any high interest rate environment to lock in yields to better secure part of your fixed-annuity obligation. A very typical allocation for a CRAT is 55 percent equities and 45 percent bonds. A more conservative allocation is 50 percent equities and 50 percent fixed income. If you are more aggressive, a typical allocation might be 70 percent equities and 30 percent fixed income. Taking a middle-of-the-road allocation, here is one way to structure your portfolio:

Large-cap equities	25%
Mid-cap equities	10%
Small-cap equities	10%
International equities	10%
Short-term fixed income	15%
Intermediate fixed income	30%
Total	100%

With this structure, you have a balance between bonds and stocks so that half of your funds can be earmarked for achieving the annual annuity. It will be difficult to achieve your payout during low interest-rate periods, so it is important to have some funds in short-term securities that can be redeployed when rates rise.

Charitable Remainder Unitrusts

With the CRUT, you have some added investment flexibility because you can add assets to this trust at any time. Accordingly, you can respond to or even anticipate changing market conditions. The CRUT is revalued annually for setting the distribution. Accordingly, market value changes will affect your payout positively, as well as negatively. Nevertheless, on balance, you should invest these funds for future growth, as you will benefit not only yourself, but also the charitable beneficiary. The CRUT offers you the ability to vary the asset classes you use as compared to the CLAT. Before looking at potential asset allocation possibilities, consider some of the following investment options:

- Real estate is sometimes a good asset class to include because of its income and capital appreciation potential. Furthermore, some real estate may not pay much income but may have great appreciation potential. This could be ideal for one of the CRUT variations, such as the NIMCRUT or the Flip Unitrust. Assuming you do not need the income currently but would like to have it when you retire and are in a lower tax bracket, you can allow the funds to appreciate in the CRUT until you sell it and reinvest the funds.

- Closely held corporate stock can work in the right circumstances. It is especially appealing if the company is sold in the future. While current income may not be great, if anything at all, you can again allow the principal to appreciate until some future event, at which time you can reinvest the monies to achieve your income, investment, and charitable goals.

- Another investment possibility in the NIMCRUT is to purchase an annuity, which builds cash on a deferred-tax basis. Again, with this investment, you can control the future flow of income back to you.

- Finally, the CRUT and its variations are good vehicles to just retain some of your company stock until you want to sell it. If it appreciates, your annual cash flow will increase. When you sell it, you will not incur a capital gain until funds are actually distributed to you.

We are now ready to look at some asset allocation possibilities. It's interesting to consider different scenarios:

1. We will look at a straight CRUT with just a diversified portfolio of marketable securities.
2. We then look at a NIMCRUT or Flip Unitrust that has real estate.
3. We will then look at keeping some of your company stock in the portfolio. The idea with #2 and #3 is to show how you may wish to allocate assets around these investments.

In the table below we display these allocations The column numbers correspond to the above descriptions.

Alternative CRUT Allocations

	Straight CRUT (1)	NIMCRUT/ Flip (2)	NIMCRUT/ Flip (3)
Equities			
- Large cap	25%	20%	10%
- Mid cap	15	10	0
- Small cap	15	10	0
- International	10	5	10
- Company stock	0	0	50
Fixed Income			
- Short term	10	10	10
- Intermediate	25	20	20
Real Estate	0	25	0
Total	100%	100%	100%

Here is a possible rationale for this game plan:

- With portfolio #1, we suggest a higher equity weighting than we did for the CRAT because of the annual revaluation and the possibilities to increase future cash flow.

- In portfolio #2, we assume a 25 percent real estate allocation. We balance some fixed income around it but take most of the allocated funds from equities, as we would look at the real estate more for growth.

- In portfolio #3, where you have your company stock, we assume you are contributing closely held company stock and that it would fill the space of mid- to small-cap equity. That is why we eliminated allocations to those sectors. On the other hand, if you are contributing a publicly traded large-cap stock, we would retain some small- and mid-cap exposure and perhaps reduce the large-cap and international allocations.

Charitable Lead Trusts

With the roles reversed from the CRT, the investment strategies will also modify to accomplish a different set of financial objectives. First, we need to remember there are two types of charitable lead trusts. One is a grantor lead trust, in which the donor gets an upfront charitable income tax deduction, but is then taxed on the annual income whether it is distributed to charity or not. The donor does not receive any further deductions beyond the initial one. The investment implications are as follows:

- To the extent possible and as long as it is consistent with the overall investment strategy, municipal bonds should be part of the portfolio to minimize the impact of income taxes on the grantor.

- If the trust is no longer a grantor lead trust because the grantor died or because of other legal circumstances, part of the original income tax deduction is recaptured by the IRS. The precise amount is the difference between the original deduction and the amounts actually paid to charity. The numbers are adjusted to account for the proper present values.

The second CLT type is the non-grantor trust where the donor receives no upfront income tax deduction, but also has no ongoing tax liability. In this case, the trust itself is subject to income taxation, unlike the charitable remainder trust. However, the CLT receives a complete charitable income tax deduction for funds disbursed to charities in that given year. Consequently, any earned income that is not disbursed to charity in a given year will be subject to taxes with no right of carry-forwards. This leads to the question of the pattern of the annuity payments. To mitigate any potential detrimental tax liabilities, the CLAT document should specify that distributions occur in the following order:

1. Ordinary income, including short-term gains
2. Long-term capital gain
3. Unrelated business income
4. Tax-exempt income
5. Return of capital

Another feature of the charitable lead trust is the opportunity to pass wealth to the next generation. To the extent that you can outperform the federal AFR, that excess will flow to your heirs free of estate and gift taxes. This can have significant investment implications.

We will now look at some specific strategies for the CLAT and CLUT, respectively.

Charitable Lead Annuity Trust

From an investment perspective, the charitable lead annuity trust creates a firm performance obligation while presenting a significant wealth transfer opportunity. The annuity distribution can change annually, but the amount must be readily discernable in advance. For instance, you can specify that the annuity can increase by 20 percent annually. Consequently, you need to ensure that the trust has either enough annual income or enough growth to fulfill that obligation over the long term. You essentially determine how challenging it will be to accomplish your investment objectives by setting the payout rate, term, and/or remainder interest. For example, having a "zeroed-out" CLAT puts pressure on your payout rate. One way to position the CLAT to accomplish your objectives is to have an increasing-annuity CLAT, as we discussed earlier, and set the initial rate lower than you otherwise might. Nevertheless, here is a possible allocation for a CLAT in which you have a moderate annual payout, perhaps in the 6 percent range.

Large-cap equities	20%
Mid-cap equities	10%
Small-cap equities	10%
International equities	10%
Short-term bonds	20%
Intermediate bonds	30%
Total	100%

This allocation balances growth with income to manage the cash flow needed to meet the annual payout, realizing that you will still need to sell assets to get the 6 percent distribution.

There is one footnote to the investment strategy. If you name your grandchildren as the remainder beneficiaries, any investment returns in excess of the present value of the remainder interest will not totally escape the generation-skipping tax. To illustrate, the remainder interest is first calculated to grow at the applicable federal AFR. To the extent that the remainder interest grows in excess of that value, some GST tax will be paid. Accordingly, if you wish to name your grandchildren as beneficiaries of a charitable lead trust, you are better off doing so under a CLUT, which we will cover next.

Charitable Lead Unitrusts

Again, the unitrust structure provides enhanced investment possibilities, since the trust is revalued annually. With the CLUT, you cannot structure it to zero out for gift tax purposes, but you can get it fairly low. Also, any appreciation is shared with the charity, as its annual payout will be a function of the revalued asset base. A significant benefit over the CLAT is that when you have grandchildren as remaindermen, any performance in excess of the original present value will pass to them free of estate and gift taxes.

As a result, the investment strategy inside a CLUT can be slightly more aggressive in an effort to build value for your heirs as well as increase the asset base for charitable distributions. You may also want to contribute and manage your concentrated stock position in this vehicle, particularly if you are bullish on the company's prospects. Furthermore, you can sell at any time without tax consequences to you if the trust is a non-grantor trust. Here is a suggested allocation using traditional asset classes:

Large-cap stocks	30%
Mid-cap stocks	15%
Small-cap stocks	10%
International stocks	5%
Emerging market stocks	5%
Short-term bonds	10%
Intermediate-term bonds	25%
Total	100%

Donor Advised Funds

Providers of donor advised funds will offer participants a series of mutual funds, along with suggestions on how to allocate your funds among them. They also tend to combine funds within specific strategies to assist investors in this process. To illustrate a sample offering, we constructed a range of portfolio alternatives displayed in the table on the following page. The individual strategies can be categorized as follows:

1. *Capital preservation:* This portfolio set offers very little principal risk to either credit losses or interest rate movements.

2. *Current income:* This strategy emphasizes high current income, but will carry some interest rate risk. Principal values will fluctuate with changes in interest rates.

3. *Growth and income:* This strategy begins to introduce equities, but emphasizes funds that invest in convertible securities and high-

dividend stocks. It will also continue to maintain a dominant weighting in fixed income.

4. *Balanced:* Here we have a fairly equal weighting in equity and fixed-income investments. We also begin to introduce additional equity classes, such as mid- and small-cap funds.

5. *Growth:* The emphasis shifts decisively toward equity investments, along with an expansion in equity asset classes.

6. *Aggressive growth:* This strategy is essentially an all-equity approach.

Asset Classes	Capital Preservation	Current Income	Growth & Income	Balanced	Growth	Aggressive
Cash reserves	50%	20%	10%	5%	0%	0%
Short-term bonds	50	30	20	15	10	0
Intermed. Bonds	0	50	30	25	20	0
Convertible securities	0	0	25	10	10	20
Large cap stocks	0	0	15	20	25	35
Mid cap stocks	0	0	0	10	15	15
Small cap stocks	0	0	0	10	10	15
Internat'l stocks	0	0	0	5	10	15
Total	100%	100%	100%	100%	100%	100%

Private Family Foundations

We capstone our investment discussion with a comprehensive review of how significant private foundations design, implement, and monitor their investment programs. The trustees or directors of private foundations have a fiduciary obligation to properly oversee the management of the foundation's portfolio. They are generally accountable to the communities the foundation serves, but in many states, they are also accountable to the state's attorney general. It is common to find language similar to the following when describing the role of fiduciaries:

> "The Portfolio shall be invested in compliance with the Prudent Investor Rule under which fiduciaries must adhere to the fundamental fiduciary duties of loyalty, impartiality and

prudence. Fiduciaries must strive to maintain overall portfolio risk at a reasonable level. Risk and return objectives must be reasonable and suitable to the Foundation's needs; provide for the reasonable diversification of portfolio assets; act with prudence in deciding whether and how to delegate authority to experts; and be cost conscious when investing."

Before getting into the actual investment process, the foundation trustees need to make some high-level decisions regarding the governance of the process. They usually have four alternatives:

1. They can manage the process themselves through the foundation manager, an in-house chief investment officer, or a designated trustee. They would undertake the role of setting objectives, establishing asset allocation targets, conducting manager searches, and monitoring/rebalancing the portfolios.

2. They can hire an independent investment consultant or consulting firm whose sole business is providing asset allocation, manager search, and performance monitoring services to foundations, endowments, pension funds, and high-net-worth individuals. They sell no products directly.

3. Along the lines of hiring an investment consultant, you can engage the services of an investment banking firm that offers a complete advisory service encompassing asset allocation, manager search, portfolio monitoring, custody, trading, reporting, and, in some cases, even tax and estate planning.

4. You can hire one firm to manage all of the money internally, with its own proprietary funds. Large foundations generally do not follow this path anymore, as they want their assets diversified among several money managers.

Regardless of which approach is taken, the same general process needs to take place to put a solid plan into place. In Figure 11 we show schematically how the process unfurls. We will consider each step in turn.

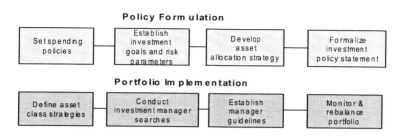

Figure 11
Investment Planning Process

Policy Formulation

| Set spending policies | Establish investment goals and risk parameters | Develop asset allocation strategy | Formalize investment policy statement |

Portfolio Implementation

| Define asset class strategies | Conduct investment manager searches | Establish manager guidelines | Monitor & rebalance portfolio |

Policy Formulation

Set Spending Policies

Regardless of what goes on in the financial markets, your foundation has some important hurdles to overcome. These hurdles are contained in what is termed the foundation's spending policy, which then becomes an integral part of the investment objectives. Here are the components of a typical spending policy:

- *Annual payout:* This is the 5 percent statutory payout ratio. As this needs to be paid, it becomes the baseline performance bogey, regardless of market conditions.

- *Administrative expenses:* A foundation has a range of expenses, including the director's salary and that of other staff. Generally, these expenses will be 1 percent to 2 percent of the asset base.

- *Inflation:* Most foundations also want to achieve a premium in their returns to cover inflation.

- *Real growth:* To be in a position to meet increasing demands and opportunities, most foundations do not just want to meet costs. Like any business, they want some "profit," or growth, in their asset base.

Establish Investment Goals and Risk Parameters

For a significant portfolio, developing investment goals is no longer as simple as saying you want to beat the market. There are a number of ways to define investment goals, and, as we will discuss below, there are also a number of ways to categorize investment risk.

Let's first look at some of the methods for quantifying your goals:

1. Continuing our earlier discussion on spending policies, consider the following example with numbers attached:

Annual payout	5%
Administrative expenses	1%
Inflation	2%
Real growth	1%
Target return	9%

2. Another way to establish investment goals is to determine a realistic premium over the risk-free rate of return. This risk-free rate is usually the treasury bill return. For example, you may state your objective as being 4 percent above the risk-free return over a full market cycle.

3. To deal with abnormal time periods, some investment advisers are beginning to measure performance over what is termed "rolling periods." Here, for instance, you measure returns over rolling five-year periods to get a better idea of how consistent your results are against the benchmarks.

4. In addition to an overall portfolio return, some entities will move more deeply into the portfolio to establish goals for each asset class to ensure it is being properly compensated for the level of risk taken. Here is an example of how you might construct these sub-level objectives:

Total portfolio	T-Bills plus 4%
Large-cap equity	T-Bills plus 5%
Mid-cap equity	T-Bills plus 6%
Small-cap equity	T-Bills plus 7%
International equity	T-Bills plus 6%
Fixed income	T-Bills plus 2%

5. Finally, your foundation's investment goal can be articulated in terms of a risk-adjusted return, which, as the name implies, adjusts your gross return for the level of risk inherent in your portfolio.

We next turn to understanding the various ways any portfolio can incur investment risk. Perhaps the best place to start is to define risk, since it can be defined in many ways. Risk is:

- The loss of value of a security, of an asset class, or of the aggregate portfolio
- The volatility in the return of an asset, sector, or the entire portfolio
- Failing to achieve the portfolio's stated objective
- Allocating funds to out-of-favor asset classes
- Managers under-performing their benchmarks

For foundations the primary risk factors are:

- Maintaining sufficient liquidity for annual distributions
- Achieving a total return that will allow the foundation's assets to grow net of distributions and inflation
- Achieving the proper diversification to minimize the fluctuations of its principal value

While foundations certainly invest for the long term, they are not in a great position to tolerate large short-term swings, and their operation is not suited to withstand a multi-year bear market without significantly cutting back on contributions. The 5 percent annual payout is calculated on the average balances of the prior year. Accordingly, in down years, the foundation either cuts back on grants or cuts into its capital if it wants to maintain a certain grant level. The investment implications are that some effort must be made to balance the peaks and valleys while achieving a long-term target return.

Develop Asset Allocation Strategy

Many investment experts will tell you that asset allocation is perhaps the most critical decision one makes when investing. In fact, some studies claim asset allocation accounts for 80 percent to 90 percent of a portfolio's return. Regardless of the percentage, asset allocation is indeed important.

Asset allocation comes in two versions: strategic and tactical. Strategic asset allocation, as the name implies, is the process of mixing a range of different assets in a portfolio, in varying proportions, to achieve a long-term investment goal within a measured level of risk. The actual process entails assigning a target weight for each major asset and asset class. A band is then developed around each asset class, indicating a minimum and maximum range for each asset category. The initial allocations are set at the target weights. Market forces, appreciation or depreciation of assets, as well as income will change the relative weights of the assets in the portfolio. Accordingly, when the weight of an asset moves beyond its target bands, you should rebalance it to its target allocation.

Strategic asset allocation is therefore a disciplined approach, making no market timing bets on specific asset classes. Adhering to this discipline may require you to sell assets that have appreciated and buy assets that are depressed. It may be difficult for some investors to adhere to this "contrarian" philosophy. Over long periods of time, however, such strategic asset allocation ensures sufficient diversification and mitigates the risk of vanishing profits.

We should say a word or two about tactical asset allocation, which involves adjusting your portfolio allocations to take advantage of short-term opportunities or to avoid perceived short-term risks. An opportunity could be present in the form of over-weighting large-cap stocks during a world crisis that you are fairly confident will be resolved positively.. A short-term market risk could be rapidly rising interest rates, and you wish to avoid bonds until the market settles. Some investors avoid tactical asset allocation, while others seem to practice it aggressively.

When actually developing your asset allocation strategy, you will first need to identify the range of asset classes you are willing to invest in. The following two tables show examples of the different asset classes by major asset category and a similar breakdown for hedge funds. The major asset categories include cash equivalents, fixed income, equity and alternative investments. A sample breakdown of these major categories is as follows:

Cash

- Commercial Paper
- US Treasury Bills
- U.S. Agencies
- Master Notes
- Weekly Floaters
- Bankers Acceptances
- Tax anticipation Notes

Fixed Income

- Corporate Bonds
- U.S. Treasury Bonds
- Municipal Bonds
- U.S. Agency Bonds
- International Bonds
- High yield Bonds
- Mortgage –Backed Bonds

Equity

- Large Cap Stock

Alternatives

- Real Estate

- Mid Cap Stock
- Small Cap Stock
- International Stocks
- Emerging Market Stocks
- Convertible Securities

- Private Equity
- Hedge Funds
- Timber
- Oil & Gas
- Venture Capital

Hedge funds can also be looked at by category or style. There are different ways to review hedge funds but here is one way:

Lower Volatility

- Market Neutral
- Equity Hedge
- Convertible Arbitrage
- Event Driven

Higher Volatility

- Long-Short Directional
- Short Selling
- Distressed Securities
- Technology
- Emerging Markets

You will then want to understand the return/risk profile for each asset category. There are three statistical measures to consider: expected return, standard deviation, and correlation:

The *expected return* is a long-term projection based predominately on historical results, but it can be tweaked by the user to adjust for anticipated patterns in the future. More importantly, one should also understand that historical results never guarantee future results.

The *standard deviation* is a recognized measure of volatility in the returns. One standard deviation is said to explain 68 percent of the return, while two standard deviations represent 95 percent of the return. For example, if an asset class is expected to return 10 percent over the long run with a standard deviation of 8 percent, you would expect that 68 percent of the time, its return will fall between 2 percent and 18 percent.

To illustrate these numerical relationships, consider the table below, where we show a range of asset classes with an expected return and standard deviation. These numbers are shown for illustration purposes only and should not be relied upon to make your personal investment decisions. You need to consult with your investment adviser for up-to-date and reliable figures. The point we are trying to show is the relationship among the various asset categories.

Asset Class	Expected Return	Standard Deviation
Cash	3.0%	1.3%
Investment-grade bonds	6.5%	7.0%
Large-cap stocks	9.0%	16.0%
Mid-cap stocks	10.5%	18.0%
Small-cap stocks	12.0%	20.0%
International stocks	10.0%	19.5%
High-yield bonds	8.5%	9.2%
Real estate	7.0%	5.0%
Private equity	12.0%	17.5%
Hedge funds – low volatility	11.5%	10.2%
Hedge funds – directional	19.5%	20.5%

In addition to looking at the expected return and standard deviation, an investor will want to be aware of the concept of *correlation,* which measures the degree to which the performance of two asset classes tend to move together. For example, if two asset classes do not move in tandem, by combining them in the same portfolio, you may actually be able to reduce the volatility of the combined portfolio compared to the volatility of the assets alone. The statistical measurement is called a correlation coefficient, which ranges between –1.0 and 1.0. A highly positive correlation (near 1.0) indicates a strong direct relationship, while a negative correlation (near-1.0) indicates a strong inverse relationship between the assets. A correlation coefficient near zero means there is relatively no relationship between the assets.

Let's consider a hypothetical situation, comparing the relationship between large-cap equities and a group of other asset classes:

Asset Class	Correlation Coefficient
Large-cap equities	1.00
Mid-cap equities	0.90
Small-cap equities	0.70
International equities	0.58
Investment-grade bonds	0.46
High-yield bonds	-0.01
Real estate	0.01
Hedge funds – low volatility	0.64
Hedge funds – directional	0.62
Private equity	0.67

This type of chart has some implications for constructing a foundation's portfolio:

- While bonds will usually lag behind stocks in an up market, they also tend to outperform in down markets, so they are an important asset class for maintaining stability in the portfolio.

- Real estate seems to move on its own and may not be closely related to the movement of the stock market. Accordingly, it can also be a good balance against financial securities.

- Hedge funds display a low correlation to the large-cap equity market and can potentially serve the portfolio well in down markets. Particular hedge funds by themselves can be quite risky, however.

To arrive at a decision on the exact mix of asset classes, your investment consultant will likely have some type of quantitative program called a portfolio optimizer. Simply stated, the optimizer combines the inputs (expected return, standard deviation, and correlation coefficient) for each designated asset class to arrive at what is called the "efficient frontier." The efficient frontier is the theoretical set of portfolios that provide the highest expected return for each level of expected risk. At this juncture, you have decided upon the asset classes you want, as well as the allocation to each.

Formalize Investment Policy Statement

Nearly all foundations, especially those with external boards, have some form of governing investment document commonly referred to as an investment policy statement. We included a sample of this document as an appendix to this chapter. It essentially contains much of the information we've covered so far, along with what we will cover in the remaining pages of this chapter.

Portfolio Implementation

We are now ready to begin the process of implementing the investment program. We will continue on with the process, covering the four remaining steps.

Define Asset Class Strategies

Within each general asset class, investors need to decide on a number of specific strategies to guide the implementation of the foundation's strategy. We will look at five asset classes that foundations actively invest in: equities, fixed income, hedge funds, real estate, and private equity. Before we do that, however, we will look at the various vehicles you can employ within each of the asset classes. Some are more appropriate than others for investing in particular asset classes.

Mutual funds: Today there are probably as many mutual funds as there are securities to purchase, so your options are abundant. For certain asset categories, mutual funds will be the most efficient choice, such as with international equity. It is difficult to arrange for custody and reporting services for this asset (unless you have a portfolio of American Depository Receipts), so trying to have a portfolio of individual securities can be cumbersome. One of the issues will be cost. The management fees in mutual funds are fixed for everyone.

Exchange-traded funds: One of the fastest growing vehicles, exchange traded funds are like index funds. Underlying these vehicles are portfolios that are passively managed to track a market index or sector. The funds are also trade daily on securities exchanges, and they carry relatively low expense ratios.

Individual securities: This is the traditional portfolio, consisting of individual securities, managed by a professional money manager. This is generally the most popular vehicle, since it is the most customizable.

Limited partnerships: Some investments are best suited for the limited partnership structure. In particular, alternative investments, such as hedge funds, private equity, and real estate, are offered this way.

Wrap programs: These are comprehensive programs entailing asset allocation, manager search, and portfolio monitoring, along with trading and reporting. Each program is generally offered at one "wrap" fee.

We will now look at each of the asset classes:

Equities: In addition to deciding to invest in mid- and small-cap stocks, as well as large-cap, you may also need to determine the particular style of management you want. This can make a significant difference in any given year. In each of the years 2000 and 2001, one of the highest performing asset classes was small-cap value with market index returns of 22.83 percent in 2000 and 14.02 percent in 2001. One of the lowest performing asset classes was small-cap growth, with a return of -22.43 percent in 2000 and -9.23 percent in 2001. If we back up to 1999, one of the best performing asset classes was small-cap growth at 43.09 percent, with small-cap value coming in as one of the worst performing classes at -1.49 percent. (The source of these statistics is Frontier Analytics, Inc., and Ibbotson Associates, Inc.)

Accordingly, a key asset class decision is what investment styles you want within each class. Management styles include value, growth, and core, which is a blended style encompassing value and growth stocks. Selecting multiple styles increases diversification in a foundation's portfolio, further mitigating the performance peaks and valleys. On the other hand, you won't want a proliferation of styles, as they will become unwieldy.

Another asset class alternative is to use index funds or indexed portfolios. Foundations sometimes use S&P 500 index funds as a proxy for their large-cap allocation. Some common benefits of indexing are predictable performance against the benchmark, low expense ratios, and immediate liquidity. One of its principal benefits, however, is not relevant for foundations. This is the low turnover in the funds. For taxable investors, low turnover means low capital gains, and foundations are tax-exempt, except for the 2 percent excise tax.

Fixed income: With bonds, your asset class decisions revolve around the following:

- Do you want an active manager or a passive manager? An active manager will actively trade bonds and manage for a total return, including capital gains and income. A passive manager will essentially ladder the maturities in the portfolio and hold the bonds until maturity. They generally maintain a portfolio with an intermediate-term average maturity; whereas, an active manager will vary the maturities.

- Do you want specialist managers, such as a mortgage-backed or international bond manager?

- Are you interested in a high-yield bond manager or a convertible bond manager? These are actually quasi-equity managers.

Hedge funds: The first key decision you face with this asset class is how you wish to access it. You generally have three ways to do so:

1. You can purchase an individual fund. This approach certainly allows you to select the specific fund you want to be in, but there are also many disadvantages to this approach. First, hedge funds usually have high minimums. Individual funds may have long notice periods for redemption. Also, an individual fund may employ a concentrated strategy, which at any time may be in or out of favor. This could negate an important reason for getting into these investments.

2. You can develop a portfolio of hedge funds yourself. This is not a bad strategy if you have substantial assets to commit. Usually, you

need at least $10 million to think about going this route. While you gain more diversification than employing the strategy above, you have the job of conducting due diligence and monitoring. This is a difficult task, as hedge funds are largely unregulated, although it is likely the SEC will begin doing so at some point.

3. You can go into a fund of funds, which invests in a variety of hedge funds across a spectrum of strategies. Advantages include significant diversification and due diligence monitoring. Disadvantages commonly include an added expense layer and the inability to customize it.

When investing in hedge funds, you are able to distinguish between two general styles and can sometimes allocate monies between them.

- A certain class of funds is categorized as *market neutral*, where the major objective is to greatly reduce market risk. The funds do this by investing equally in long- and short-equity portfolios generally in the same sectors of the market. An example of a specific transaction is buying a convertible bond and selling short the underlying stock. This is known as a convertible arbitrage strategy. The performance objective is to achieve a targeted range of absolute returns. Some investors use these funds as bond surrogates.

- A more aggressive approach is in directional hedge funds. Here the managers take directional bets on the market or sectors of a market.

It is certainly beyond the scope of this book to go much more into the mechanics of hedge funds, but it is important to note why they have become very popular, particularly among foundations and endowments. As foundations have annual payout requirements and may have committed to multi-year programs, they need to have some assurance that the returns have an element of consistency. Hedge funds, because of their low correlation to traditional stock and bond portfolios, offer some of the diversification that allows foundations to balance the ups and downs of the market. Foundations, in the long run, need to shoot for strong absolute returns as much as they need to peg market benchmarks. Slightly beating the benchmark in down markets does not necessarily pay the bills.

Private equity: Here you have three different ways to invest.

1. First, you can make a series of direct investments in single companies, keeping in mind that you risk having unrelated business income, and you are restricted as to your total ownership percentage. The appeal of this approach is that you can select your own

investments. But you also may end up with concentrated investments without adequate diversification.

2. A second way to invest is to select private equity and venture capital funds that, in turn, hold investments in a series of individual companies. This does give you some diversification, and there is also a managing partner overseeing the investments.

3. A third way is to invest in a fund of funds that includes investments in a group of private equity funds. This type of investment can provide investments in many companies across a number of industries. You also have the benefit of a managing partner and staff who provide due diligence and oversight. This does, however, add another layer of fees.

Foundations will generally opt for alternatives two or three. Unless one of the trustees is proficient in the private equity arena, foundations may be best served by the fund-of-funds approach to obtain the necessary level of oversight.

Real estate: This asset class also offers a number of ways to invest. Again, you can invest directly in specific real estate deals but need to watch for unrelated business income if the properties have debt. You can also access different types of real estate funds and partnerships. Some funds feature large office buildings with income and cash flow. Others feature a diversified mixture of mid-size commercial and residential properties. Still other funds may be more opportunistic in that they will purchase properties that require upgrading. Real estate investment offers foundations diversification and low volatility. As the above table on correlation shows, real estate enjoys a low correlation to the stock market. Its market value also tends to display low volatility. In recent years, an off-shoot to real estate has emerged. This involves investments in timber properties.

Conduct Investment Manager Searches

Continuing with the implementation, you next need to decide who manages the foundation's money. While mutual funds is always an option, we will devote this section to the evaluation of private investment managers. We will first cover some pointers on how to select managers and then cover reasons why you may need to replace managers.

Selecting Managers

Performance is always high on the list, so we will start with it. We suggest that your performance review go much further than looking at the best performing manager last year, since the best in one year sometimes becomes the worst the following year. Here are some of the performance indicators you should look for when selecting a foundation money manager:

- A minimum five-year track record
- Competitive numbers against the market benchmark over a full market cycle
- Performance consistency as measured by three- and five-year rolling period analysis
- First-quartile peer-group performance over five years, with at least second-quartile over intermediate periods
- Favorable up/down market performance against the benchmark. Here we are looking for the manager to stay fairly close to the benchmark in up markets but to outperform it in down markets.
- Favorable risk-adjusted performance

You should also look at the manager's investment style and how the firm manages it. Here are some indicators:

- Does the manager stay true to his or her style, or does the firm experience style drift?
- Is the investment process dependent on one person, or is there a team of people not dependent upon any one individual?
- How extensive are the firm's investment research resources?

In addition to the firm's investment process, you should look at the firm itself and how it is managed. Some common things to look at include:

- Assets under management and growth rate over the past few years
- Relationships per investment manager
- Back-office operations
- Experience of key officers

When looking at hedge fund managers or fund-of-fund managers, you should examine some other factors, including but not limited to:

- Ownership structure and incentive compensation plans
- Capital invested by management
- Sector or fund concentrations
- Maximum short positions
- Liquidity

- Decision process

Terminating Managers

Sometimes you have the unfortunate task of terminating a manager. While the reasons many times center on performance, they don't always. A common reason for terminating a manager is the firm's being purchased or merged, and the resulting company is not to your liking. Another common reason is that a group of key officers leave the firm, and you are nervous about how the firm will recover, or you just wish to follow your portfolio manager to his or her new firm.

Establishing Manager Guidelines

A key element of investment oversight is establishing clear performance and operating guidelines for the investment managers. Generally, performance guidelines cover expected results against market benchmarks and peer groups. Also, as mentioned earlier, performance consistency and favorable risk-adjusted returns are critical to ensuring the portfolio is well positioned for volatile markets.

It is also important to have clear operating guidelines and restrictions. Among the common ones are:

- Minimum quality ratings on bonds
- Prohibited investments, such as short selling, uncovered puts and calls, margin and currency speculation
- Individual security and industry concentrations

Monitor and Rebalance Portfolios

Performance Monitoring

Market volatility has increased the need for constant monitoring of investment portfolios, particularly where multiple asset classes and managers are employed. As a fiduciary, you are likely to evaluate the following:

- Current asset allocation and variance from targets
- Market value changes over recent time period
- Performance against market benchmark and peer group
- Risk/return analysis
- Attribution analysis
- Up/down market returns
- Top 10 holdings

- Equity sector allocations
- Bond maturity and quality analysis

Portfolio Rebalancing

Rebalancing the portfolio is critical to preserving capital and maintaining a proper investment discipline. Unlike taxable portfolios, a foundation's is not taxable, so there is no compelling reason not to adhere to your strategic asset allocation targets. Generally, you will rebalance under these circumstances:

- Major asset classes (equity, fixed income, cash, and alternatives) exceed their maximum ranges.
- Sub asset classes exceed their ranges.
- You identify new asset classes to invest in.
- Market conditions radically change, and you want to react.

Critical to achieving your wealth transfer and philanthropic goals is a highly successful investment program. We spoke earlier about transferring wealth through charitable lead trusts or charitable family limited partnerships. Making these structures work is contingent upon the investment results. The higher the returns, the more money goes to your heirs estate tax free. As to the charitable beneficiaries, investment results not only need to be good, but they need to be consistent and somewhat predictable. Or at least capital needs to be preserved as much as possible during bear markets.

Chapter 8 Appendix
Sample Investment Policy Statement

SMITH FAMILY FOUNDATION

Statement of Investment Policy
June 15, 2002

Table of Contents

SMITH FAMILY FOUNDATION
Statement of Investment Policy

Overview

The scope of this document is to delineate the general operating guidelines, investment objectives, specific asset class strategies, and the process for selecting and monitoring investment managers for the Smith Family Foundation. This process involves the following steps, each of which we will cover in detail below:

1. General Operating Guidelines
2. Establishing Risk Profiles
3. Articulating Investment Objectives
4. Statement on Mission-related Investments
5. Determining Asset Classes and Allocations
6. Defining Asset Class Strategies
7. Selecting Investment Managers
8. Establishing Manager Objectives & Guidelines
9. Tracking Investment Performance
10. Terminating Investment Managers
11. Rebalancing Portfolios

General Operating Guidelines

A. The Investment Committee of the Foundation is charged with governing the investments of the Foundation's assets.
B. Specifically, it is responsible for overseeing the allocation of fund assets and selecting and monitoring the individual investment managers.
C. To assist it in executing these duties, the Investment Committee may hire a professional investment consulting organization.
D. The Investment Advisor shall submit quarterly performance reports to the Investment Committee. Additionally, individual managers will appear before the Investment Committee of the Foundation as requested by the Committee from time to time.
E. Subject to restrictions listed in these guidelines and objectives, investment managers shall have full discretion in their investment decisions.

F. As an overriding policy, no manager may make an investment which would be considered a "jeopardizing investment" under section 4944 of the Internal Revenue Code.

G. When funds are needed by the Foundation to pay grants, they will be taken on a pro rata basis from each manager.

Establishing Risk Profiles

A. Risk can be approached in a number of ways and there is not necessarily one correct way to fit all situations. Determining risk is as much an "art" as it is a "science." To therefore arrive at a statement of investment risk for the portfolio, we consider the relative importance of each of these factors.

- Desire for high total return
- Desire for long-term capital growth
- Need for high level of income
- Ability to tolerate principal fluctuations
- Ability to suffer a loss in any single year
- Need for liquidity
- Willingness to invest with an "out of favor" asset class and manager.

B. The primary risk factors for the foundation are: maintaining sufficient liquidity for annual distributions, achieving a total return that will allow the Foundation's assets to grow net of distributions and inflation, and diversifying the investments to minimize the fluctuations of the principal value.

C. The Foundation also maintains certain attitudes toward the assumption of risk. These attitudes, as expressed below, will provide guidance to the Investment Advisor and Managers alike:

- The Foundation is willing to sacrifice some opportunities for gain during rising markets in order to avoid large potential losses during declining markets

- The Foundation is willing to accept market risk with its traditional equity and fixed income managers. The foundation is averse to the firm-specific risk associated with companies whose survival is in question. Non-investment grade-rated securities and equity investments in such companies are not encouraged by traditional equity and fixed income managers.

- The Investment Committee adheres to the capital market theory which maintains that over the very long term, the risk of owning equities should be rewarded with a somewhat greater return than available from fixed income investments. Consequently, the asset allocation policy allows a higher concentration in equity securities as a means of enhancing portfolio returns over the long term.

- Notwithstanding the above statements, the Investment Committee may allocate a percentage of its assets into alternative investments *(e.g.,* private equity, hedge funds and real estate) if it feels that the impact would be meaningful to future returns and the portfolio's risk profile. It realizes that alternative investment managers would not be subject to some of the same guidelines as the traditional managers.

- The Investment Committee will manage its overall risk through asset allocation and investment manager styles.

Articulating Investment Objectives

A. Using the risk profile as a basis, we then establish general investment objectives for the Foundation. These objectives address the relative importance of distributions, income, preservation of principal, capital growth, and liquidity.

B. Over a five year period, the Foundation desires to achieve a real rate of return in excess of its Spending Policy. In today's environment, the Spending Policy is as follows:

Annual payout	5.00%
Administrative expenses	0.25%
Inflation	2.50%
Real growth	1.50%
Target return	9.25%

C. The Committee wants to achieve this return at the optimal level of risk. Accordingly, the target risk levels (as measured by the standard deviation) should range from 9 to 12%.

Statement on Mission-Related Investments

A. The Foundation's investment managers will exclude from the investment portfolio all stocks and bonds of companies engaged in the manufacture of tobacco products, alcohol, and handguns.

B. The Foundation Trustees may elect to allocate some of its assets into program related investments as part of its philanthropic strategy.

Determining Asset Classes and Allocations

A. Tempering the investment objectives with the Foundation's risk profile, we derived the general asset classes we wish to employ to implement the investment program. Providing background for these decisions, we employed a quantitative evaluation of alternative portfolio allocations taking into account an asset class' projected return, its projected volatility and correlation with other asset classes. The major asset classes are equities, fixed income and cash equivalents as well as alternative investments encompassing private equity, real estate and hedge funds.

B. Through this optimization process, the Foundation arrived at the following overall target allocation on a consolidated basis:

	Minimum	Target	Maximum
Cash equivalents	0	1	5
Fixed income	20	25	40
Equities	40	55	65
Real estate	6	7	10
Alternative investments	0	12	15

C. Drilling down further, we have established general consolidated guidelines for the sub-asset classes as well:

	Minimum	Target	Maximum
Cash equivalents	0	1	5
Fixed income			

-Preferred	0	3	5
-Investment grade (corp/gov)	15	20	30
-Municipal	0	0	15
-Convertible	0	2	5
Equities			
-Large cap	25	30	45
-Mid cap	0	8	10
-Small cap	0	5	8
-International	10	10	15
-Emerging markets	0	2	4

	Minimum	Target	Maximum
Alternative investments			
-Hedge funds	0	6	10
-Private equity	0	4	8
-High yield	0	2	5
Real estate			
-REITs	6	7	10

Defining Asset Class Strategies

Within each asset class, there is a specific strategy as delineated below:

Equities

1. There are two major segments to the equity portion-core and specialty.
2. The core segment encompasses the large cap components and is further segmented between value and growth styles. Managers will be hired to focus on a specific style. Alternatively, the Foundation could hire a core large cap manager that follows a blended style.

3. The specialty segment encompasses the following asset classes:

    a. Small cap equity
    b. Mid cap equity
    c. International equity
    d. Emerging markets
    e. Focused equity

    Managers could be hired in each of these categories to follow a growth, value or blended style.

4. For each asset class, we may elect to either hire individual managers, participate in a limited partnership, or purchase mutual funds.

Fixed Income

1. The purpose of fixed income is to provide current income and preserve principal value. As well, it should keep down the volatility or risk of the portfolios. Therefore, it should be managed to achieve an optimal level of current income as opposed to "total return."

2. The fixed income segment can be delivered through the following asset classes:

    a. Investment Grade Bonds (Taxable Corporate & U.S. Government)
    b. Preferred Stock
    c. Convertible Bonds
    d. Municipal Bonds (specialty)

Cash Equivalents

1. The liquidity would be maintained in a money market mutual fund.

2. Where cash balances in the Foundation's operating account become large, our strategy is to invest out on the yield curve up to two years.

3. We should take advantage of opportunities to invest in commercial paper, variable rate demand notes, corporate put bonds and dutch auction rate securities.

Alternative Investments

1. The alternative investment asset classes the Foundation will invest in are:

   a. Hedge Funds
   b. Private Equity
   c. Hi-Yield Bonds
   d. Real Estate

2. The purpose of alternative investments is to promote diversification by combining low correlated assets to the portfolio. Alternative investments, depending on the unique characteristics of each class, may lower risk, increase expected return, and / or generate income.

3. For hedge funds and private equity, the Committee will generally favor a fund of funds approach so as to achieve adequate diversification among investment types as well as among investment managers.

Selecting Investment Managers

A. Managers would be hired by asset class and specific style. We expect them to always adhere to their specific style.

B. When selecting managers the Investment Committee will consider both performance and qualitative factors. The performance factors could include but not be limited to:

- Five-year track record
- Rolling period analysis
- Risk-adjusted returns
- Downside analysis
- Style analysis & consistency
- Index & peer group benchmark comparisons

C. The qualitative factors beyond performance could include:

- Firm's ownership structure
- Key personnel
- Investment philosophy & process
- Asset growth rate
- Business model
- Administrative resources & client servicing capabilities
- Attribution analysis

Establishing Manager Objectives & Guidelines

A. Traditional Equity Managers

1. Outperform the specified, relevant market benchmark over a full market cycle or five years. Also, managers will be compared to peer groups and will be expected to perform at certain levels.

2. The funds shall be diversified. Permitted securities may include common stocks, preferred stocks, convertible debentures, corporate bonds, commercial paper, U.S. Treasury and federal agency obligations and short-term money market funds.

3. However, each portfolio should be invested primarily in equities. The manager is authorized to use cash equivalents and fixed income investments; however, the entire portfolio performance will be measured against a relevant equity benchmark.

4. No more than 10% of each portfolio at cost, or 15% at market, shall be invested in any one company.

5. While we are not mandating any specific sector or industry weightings, the Committee requests that the managers exercise prudence in the degree to which they will overweight a particular sector or industry relative to its measured benchmark.

6. Managers (handling separate accounts) are not permitted to invest in mutual funds where they are acting as an advisor unless those assets are excluded from the standard management fee or the mutual fund advisory fee is rebated.

7. Managers should not invest in mutual funds that require front- or back-end loads.

8. Managers are not permitted to conduct the following activities:

- Trading in naked options
- Short sales or trading on margin
- Purchase of commodities

B. Fixed Income Managers

1. Achieve a total rate of return that exceeds the specified benchmark. Secondary objectives include preserving capital, maintaining a high degree of liquidity, and maximizing income. Additionally, managers may be compared to peer groups.

2. Corporate bonds at the time of purchase shall be limited to investment-grade instruments rated BBB-/Baa3 or better by both Standard & Poor and Moody. Rule 144a securities are permissible but shall be limited to no more than 10% of the portfolio.

3. There is no limit on the use of U.S. Government or Agency obligations.

4. No single company shall constitute more than 10% of the total fund at time of purchase.

5. Commercial paper should be rated A-1, P-1 by Standard & Poor or Moody.

6. Certificates of Deposit shall be limited to banks whose senior debt rating is A or above

7. Futures contracts and exchange traded options on futures are permitted ONLY for the purpose of hedging interest rate exposure, managing volatility exposure, managing term structure exposure, managing sector exposure, and reducing transaction costs.

8. Managers should not invest in mutual funds where they are acting as an advisor unless those assets are excluded from the standard management fee or the mutual fund advisory fee is rebated.

9. Managers should not invest in mutual funds that require a front- or back-end load.

10. Managers are not permitted to engage in the following activities:
    - Trading in naked options
    - Short sales or trading on margin

- Purchase of commodities

C. Alternative Investment Managers

1. Hedge funds are expected to provide some stability to the annual returns due to their low cross correlation to each other and to the traditional financial assets in the portfolio. Each manager must adhere to the style for which it was selected.

2. Market neutral or absolute return hedge funds are expected to achieve a spread return above Treasury Bills. Additionally, their expected risk (standard deviation) should be low.

3. Multi-strategy or directional hedge funds are expected to achieve equity-like returns, exceeding the appropriate equity index over a market cycle.

4. Real estate, venture capital and private equity investments should exceed a benchmark of peer group investments in the marketplace.

Tracking Investment Performance

A. Investment Advisor to prepare quarterly reports.

B. Investment Advisor to conduct ongoing due diligence of managers.

C. The investment time horizon for each manager is either a full market cycle or five years, with the recent three-year performance also being important.

D. Investment Advisor to review manager attribution analysis and risk adjusted returns.

E. Investment Advisor to also measure rolling three year returns.

Terminating Investment Managers

While the foundation reserves the right to terminate any investment manager relationship at any time, it would generally do so under the following circumstances:

A. Investment performance is significantly below established benchmarks and has been for an extended time period. Moreover, the reasons for underperformance are not convincing.

B. Failure of a manager to follow his or her prescribed style

C. Violation of investment guidelines

D. Significant personnel departures from the organization

E. Change in ownership of the organization

F. Significant changes in the foundation's investment strategy

Rebalancing the Portfolio

A. When maximum asset allocation targets are exceeded, the portfolios will generally be rebalanced.

B. Some rebalancing may also take place for liquidity and tactical considerations to take advantage of changing market conditions.

    C. Generally, this Investment Policy Statement and the Foundation's asset allocation structure will be thoroughly reviewed annually.

NINE

CHARTING YOUR COURSE:
DEVELOPING YOUR CORPORATE AND PERSONAL GRANT-MAKING PROGRAM

The first two phases of developing your philanthropic plan – establishing charitable structures and managing the investments – have a lot of math and science to them, along with a little art. In this third phase, while we will certainly attempt to suggest a number of structural techniques, you are dealing predominately with art and values. Through your grant-making, you promulgate your corporate and personal family values.

For many, this is the fun part. Family foundations can evolve into an important educational, spiritual, and social focus for the family. It can be the central vehicle for perpetuating a family culture across the generations. But effective philanthropy requires a great amount of skill today. Without question, you still need to continue some of the "check writing" of the past. Your family won't abandon its support of your local religious institutions, hospitals, and other long-time favorite charities. And you certainly won't stop giving to your alma mater. Nevertheless, we will focus our discussions on the other part of your charitable giving.

In this chapter, we will suggest some basic processes as they relate to instituting a formal grant-making plan. In the next, we will look at some of the emerging trends in the wider field of philanthropy and suggest three unique ways corporate executives and business owners can make a difference in their communities.

We begin by looking at your personal and family grant-making programs. While we will be speaking specifically about foundation structure, these grant-making processes can apply to other structures where you have input into the distribution of funds (donor-advised fund, community foundation fund, etc.).

Governance

On of the very early governance rules you will need to consider is who makes the decisions on grant requests. Will you, the patriarch or matriarch, make the final decisions, with your children and other trustees just looking on? Or will you allow decisions to be reached by some consensus?

Some family foundations give each trustee the ability to direct a specific amount of money to charities of their choice, subject to general guidelines. Still other families establish separate funds for each child and let the children make decisions for their respective funds, maintaining a general family fund from which members make decisions collectively.

You should adopt the governing structure that works for your family – but be cautious about the autocratic approach, as your children and the external trustees could lose interest.

Mission

The glue that always holds a foundation (or any charitable fund) together is its mission. There are many ways you can express your grant-making mission, and we do not suggest that there is a perfect way. Instead, we will show you how you can ultimately arrive at your mission by selecting a sphere of influence. Here are some of the ways you can focus your activities:

Institutional

You can express your philanthropic strategy by highlighting specific institutions you wish to support in a broad way. One easy way to accomplish this is through a supporting organization, as we discussed in an earlier chapter. Let's assume, however, you do not opt for that structure and wish to take a broader approach. As an example, your primary mission may be to support the universities you, your spouse, and children attended and are willing to do it across the board in a number of programs (athletics, academics, student activities, etc.). You can even include some local schools if you attended college out of town. Or you may want to direct much of your charitable giving through a local community foundation or through the charitable arm of your religion (for example, Catholic Charities, Jewish Federations).

Community

Your focus could be a specific community. In this case, you may be willing to support a range of activities, as long as they are confined to your local geographic community. For example, you can support the arts, hunger organizations, after-school programs and other social service activities without preference to any specific one.

Cause

Many donors define their mission in terms of a cause. You may wish to focus funds on medical research for a specific illness, such as cancer, heart disease, or AIDS. Alternatively, your interest may lie in the environment, and you can fund a wide range of programs across a number of institutions.

Public Policy

While there are regulations prohibiting certain types of lobbying, foundations can focus their efforts on certain public policy issues. For example, you can focus your efforts on ex-offenders and the many problems they face upon re-entering society. Your objective can be to encourage legislation to provide more programs to deal with these issues. The Open Society Institute (Soros), for example, takes a strong interest in this issue. You might also feel strongly about medical care reform and the many issues surrounding that. When adopting public policy issues as an important part of your mission, you generally fund research studies and support other organizations dedicated to the same cause.

Individuals

You may feel the predominant impact of your efforts should be directly on individuals. Your funds could go to a variety of institutions for multiple purposes. For example, you may want to benefit mentoring programs, such as the Big Brothers and Big Sisters. A common grant is for scholarships, through which your money goes directly to individuals. Alternatively, you could donate books to the library at a senior center.

These examples are not intended to be mutually exclusive. It is common for donors to combine some of them to arrive at a mission statement. You may support health care institutions principally, but may also provide funding for related public policy.

Methods of Giving

You should also give much thought as to how you will structure your gifts. By no means should you confine yourself to one method of giving. Our intent here is to suggest the many different ways you can give and the purpose of each of your gifts. One of the things you should keep in mind is that all money is not the same in the field of philanthropy. Much of the support non-profit organizations receive is for specific purposes without any ability to deviate. Let's consider the wide range of possibilities:

- *Direct programs:* This is one of the most common grants for foundations, as funds are used on existing programs for a defined purpose with a measurable outcome.

- *Capital:* Here you are likely to support a charity that is building a new facility or purchasing equipment.

- *New venture:* This is essentially seed money for a new program. This requires more work on your part, along with accepting increased funding risk.

- *Program-related investments:* This is another way to fund new ventures. Sometimes foundations provide loans or make an equity investment in a new program or project. For example, you can provide capital to a non-profit that will lend money to people with low income to buy homes or start businesses.

- *Emergency support:* During stressful economic times or as a result of a natural disaster, an important non-profit could be experiencing severe financial strain. If the organization is critical to the community, you may wish to provide emergency funding.

- *Endowment:* Popular among universities, endowment supports research, scholarships, and faculty.

- *Capacity-building:* This entails providing support for things that will strengthen the operations of a non-profit entity. We will cover this in more depth in the next chapter.

- *Matching grants:* As the name implies, here you are willing to give significant funding for a program or capital campaign, provided the organization can raise funds from others. You may structure a gift in a way that matches dollar-for-dollar any gifts the charity can secure up to a specific dollar amount. Sometimes, donors offer an increased match – two-for-one, for example.

- *Unrestricted:* To a charity, this, of course, is the best money, as they are free to do with it as they please. They will use these funds for general operating support to cover salaries, rent, and administrative expenses.

- *Multi-year grants:* You need to determine to what extent you will engage in multi-year funding. This, of course, enables you to give higher amounts, but it also restricts flexibility in outer years.

Grant Decision Process

For organized recordkeeping, it is important to have an orderly process for approving grants. This will also foster better communications with the community organizations seeking grants. Essentially, you need to outline the chain of events to approve a grant. For example, you may allow the foundation manager, if you have one, full discretion on grants below a certain amount. You may then allow a certain number of trustees to approve grants between certain amounts, and require a full board review on grants above that limit.

Published Guidelines

Some foundations and donors publish their grant guidelines and either disseminate them widely or have them available for those who ask. Among the specifics you might include in written guidelines are:

- Purpose of the foundation
- Fields of interest
- Range of funding (program, capacity-building, capital, etc.)
- Restricted fields and funding methods
- Geographic preferences and restrictions
- Information required in proposals
- Size range of grants
- Percentage of a capital campaign or program you will fund
- Timing for decisions
- Information that must accompany all grant requests, including financial statements, 501(c)(3) letter showing tax exempt status, board listing, staff biographies, and other requirements

Assessing Grant Requests

Another discipline in managing a philanthropic program is to have a process for reviewing and assessing the strength of grant requests. Here you can make your life easy by adopting consistent guidelines and executing them consistently, as well. Here are some questions to consider as you review grant requests. These questions should help you formulate a clear process:

1. Does the request fit our mission?

2. What impact does a proposed program have on the community? Alternatively, if it is not widespread throughout the community, what impact does it have on the lives of individuals served?

3. Is the project or program credible? Is there a need for it?

4. Is the program clear, and are its budget assumptions realistic? Are the anticipated timelines realistic?

5. How capable is the organization asking for the funds? Do they have a strong track record with programs of this nature?

6. What types of risk do you see in the program?

7. Who else is funding the program, and which other foundations or agencies are they asking? What is the total funding requirement for the program or project? Is it realistic to assume the goal will be reached?

8. Is the organization doing its work with any others? Has it been effective in collaborating with other non-profit organizations?

9. If there is a capital request, how do you assess the impact it will have on the organization's future ability to operate?

10. Is a site visit required? If so, what do you expect to learn, and is it cost effective? More importantly, is it very likely we will do this project, believing a site visit will clear up some important questions?

11. Finally, is this the type of program that will enhance the community image of our foundation? Conversely, will our reputation be tarnished if the program or organization fails?

Evaluating a Non-profit Organization

Aside from valuating the merits of grant proposals, you also need to understand something about the organizations to which you are giving the money. Entire books are written on this topic, but we will highlight just a few important points for looking at an organization. We won't discuss organizations that offer services to the public for fees, such as hospitals and museums, but will focus on social service institutions that require charitable or public funding.

We will again start with the finances. You should focus on five key areas, briefly described here:

1. You can start with the *balance sheet*. Perhaps the critical line items relate to debt. Is there a mortgage on their building? What are the terms? Does the organization use any short-term lines of credit? Are

its accounts payable managed efficiently? On the asset side, are there any lingering receivables?

2. Alongside the balance sheet is the *income statement.* Of particular importance are the trends of various income and expense line items. Are there any non-recurring income or expense items? How are funds invested? How favorable are the overhead ratios compared to revenues and grants?

3. How well does the organization do at *budgeting?* Do they generate realistic budgets? What is their track record in meeting budgets?

4. How have their external *audits* gone?

5. Thoroughly dissect their *fund raising.* Organizations can receive funding from a variety of sources, and it is important to know a number of things about these sources. First, let's look at some of the potential sources of funding;

- Non-restricted individuals
- Non-restricted corporate
- General operating funds from foundations
- Affinity group solicitations
- Restricted funds from individuals
- Restricted funds from corporations
- Restricted funds from foundations
- Government programs
- Social events
- Selling services to other charities
- Rental income

You then need to go beyond the list to ask some more detailed questions. These are the same types of questions you would ask if you were "buying" the organization:

- Of the non-restricted individuals, what is the breakdown among large, middle-level, and small donors? Does any one person dominate the list? What was the largest gift in each of the last three years? How much do the top 10 donors give?

- Ask similar questions about corporate donors. For how many years have your top three corporate donors given? Is there a risk that any of them will not give next year?

- Obtain a trend report on the levels from each of the above over the past three years.
- Obtain details on the success of the social events over the past couple of years.
- What is the capacity to expand income from selling services and renting space?

Another way to evaluate a non-profit is to look at its overall organizational capacity. Among the points to consider are:

- Does it have effective management information systems to evaluate program profitability?
- Do staff members have the right level of technology to be efficient in their work?
- Do they have too many programs? Are the resources spread too thin?
- Do they have effective program evaluation processes in place? Have they ever dropped programs because of financial losses, low impact, or obsolescence?
- How strong is the CEO? What succession plan exists if the CEO leaves?
- Who is on the board? What things do they get involved with?
- How has staff turnover been? If turnover is high, what are the reasons for it?
- How does the organization do at forming alliances?

Follow-up and Evaluation

Finally, donors need to institute some form of program and organizational follow-up. Particularly when you make sizeable grants, you will want to know what has been achieved and how the organizations performed against agreed-upon benchmarks. Some foundations take this task seriously enough that they actually hire external evaluators to examine the effectiveness of a particular program.

You may also want to know who else has been funding the organization since you provided funds. Sometimes this is a good barometer for how the entity is doing because someone else is evaluating them. Certainly if the organization is gaining new dollars from substantial donors, your confidence in the entity is increased.

A valuable part of the follow-up process is that it enables your family and trustees to learn what went well and what did not. You can then adjust your process the next time and will, at a minimum, have some additional questions to ask of your grantees.

Corporate Grant-making

Your company's grant making program may have a lot of similarities to your own, but there will be differences. The company will also have alternatives not readily available to your family foundation.

First, let's look at some of the factors driving corporate grant-making.

- Of the various potential missions we discussed above, the community mission is likely to dominate for obvious reasons.

- Companies may also tend to support charities closely related to their field. For examples, health care companies support hospitals, and food companies give to hunger appeals.

- Companies favor charities for which their executives and employees volunteer in some capacity.

- Projects that carry high visibility have a good chance of attracting corporate contributions.

- It is always a good policy for companies to provide timely funding for serious community issues, such as education and job creation.

Companies also have an arsenal of ways they can contribute that many private foundations lack. This provides opportunities to collaborate with private donors, as well, in some areas:

- Your company can have a matching gift program.

- They can encourage employees to volunteer and provide them with company time off to do so.

- They can provide sponsorships for events and offer tickets to employees.

- Frequently, corporations provide in-kind contributions, such as equipment or in-house printing.

- Companies in such industries as computers can provide training for school children and low-income adults.

There are two major areas today where companies can effectively meld philanthropy with strategic business interests. These apply in a company's headquarters city or in a region where the company has a significant investment of resources:

- *Job force readiness:* Despite periods of economic weakness, companies continually face the challenge of securing well trained employees at all levels. Accordingly, sound philanthropic investments can be made in such areas as literacy, computer training, and even child care centers so that employees can reduce the stress of finding adequate facilities to care for their children during working hours.

- *Quality of community life:* Where you have a significant business investment, you certainly want that community to prosper for the purpose of enhancing your own business. At the same time, you may need your city or region to offer a quality life style to attract new employees to your firm. To accomplish both goals, you sometimes need to support programs that will bring about further economic development. Examples include expansion of a local healthcare facility, creation of a new museum or cultural center, and development of new research programs at the university.

The business of giving money away is still fun, but it does have its complications. The intent of this chapter was to provide you with some tools and processes to put some order to the task.

TEN

VENTURE PHILANTHROPY

You can't pick up a financial magazine nowadays without reading about the trillions of dollars that will be passed on to the next generation. At the same time, we are witnessing what many say are sea changes in the field of philanthropy. Some will also say the current trends are the most radical since the days of Carnegie.

We are indeed seeing real structural changes in the way philanthropy is managed. At the same time, we are also experiencing significant attitude changes by those gaining control of the purse strings. We will discuss both of these changes and suggest three alternative giving strategies that executives and business owners can adopt to make a real impact.

The overall emerging trend is a phenomenon called "venture philanthropy." As the name implies, venture philanthropy applies venture capital techniques to charitable giving. Like venture capitalists, venture philanthropists search for bold ideas and innovative leaders. They appear motivated by some of the following attitudes toward giving:

- They want to make a significant impact on "something" or "somebody." They want to know their money really did help some person or some organization in a very tangible way.

- They are not interested in just attending board meetings. Instead, they want to apply their entrepreneurial and professional skills to organizations and causes.

- They want to focus on a very limited number of "ventures" at any one time. They will put forth a great amount of effort during that time, but, like venture capitalists, they want an exit strategy so they can move on to something else.

Venture philanthropists conduct their charitable activities in a number of ways, including some of the following:

- They may target a field of interest, such as early childhood education, after-school activities, or geriatric issues. Then they either look for organizations engaged in those activities or invite organizations to submit proposals for funding.

- They may find innovative programs already in existence that appear to be great models. All that might be missing is the capital to expand them.

- They not only provide funding for a program, but generally support the organization carrying it out. All too often, an organization has an innovative model but not the infrastructure to effectively implement it. This is where the venture philanthropist can offer expertise and professional contacts to better ensure the success of the program.

- They like to look for real gaps in the community and then fund them. A classical example centered on computers and the "digital divide." Many high tech entrepreneurs funded computer training for school-age children, as well as adults.

Rather than continue with concept descriptions, let's look at some examples of how venture philanthropy has been applied.

Center for Venture Philanthropy

It is fitting to lead with an organization that lies in the cradle of venture philanthropy. Established in 1999 as a division of the Peninsula Community Foundation (San Francisco / Silicon Valley), the Center for Venture Philanthropy has pioneered some of the most innovative community and anti-poverty initiatives. Employing a venture capital model, they bring together community donors (i.e. investors), non profit leaders and CVP staff to approach social and economic issues in more innovative ways. Their operating structure is through "social venture funds". Like traditional venture capital funds, these social venture funds feature long term business plans (3 to 6 years), investments in a range of nonprofit enterprises, accountable results and an ultimate exit strategy. One of their social venture funds is the "Assets for all Alliance" which we will briefly look at in further detail. The vision of this program is based on the premise that individuals work out of poverty through education, business formation and their home ownership. Accordingly, the fund provides the means for low income families to buy a home, start a business, save for a college education or begin a retirement fund.

Structurally, the fund operates as a collaboration among a group of funders nonprofit service providers, Lenders for Community Development and Citibank. Through this program, participating low income individuals open up Individual Development Accounts and deposit a set amount of funds each month over a 2 to 3 year period until they reach a goal of $2,000. The Assets for all Alliance matches each savings account at a 2 to 1 rate up to the $2,000 goal, giving each participant a total of $6,000. At the same time, participants receive training in budgeting, banking services, credit management and overall preparation for home ownership or business. The CVP also keeps investors or funders regularly informed through quarterly performance reports and its Investment Council, which meets three times per year. The Investment Council brings together funders and nonprofit providers to review issues related to the program.

Goldman Philanthropic Partnerships

This group of donors is dedicated to finding innovative research and exceptional treatment alternatives to fight cancer and other deadly diseases. They have established a portfolio of cutting-edge medical research projects. Their business model is implemented through Inspired Ventures, which are charitable enterprises consisting of researchers, donors, and scientific partnerships.

Venture Philanthropy Partners

This group was founded in 1999 by three individuals in the Washington, D.C., area. The ideas came from Mario Morino, founder of Morino Institute and co-founder of LEGENT Corporation. Joining him were Raul Fernandez, founder of Proxicom, and Mark Warner, later to be governor of Virginia. Their focus is on the developmental and educational needs of low-income children in the Capital Region. Their approach is to find organizations with very compelling models and visionary leaders. They then provide significant technical and managerial assistance to those organizations. Among their priorities are building strong management teams, creating effective boards, instituting sound service delivery models, and developing appropriate information systems. From a structural standpoint, they are organized as a supporting organization to the Community Foundation of the National Capital Region.

Blue Ridge Foundation

This New York foundation focuses on start-up organizations that connect children and families in high-poverty communities to opportunities and resources on the outside. They particularly favor organizations that deal with youth development, community building, and the use of technology. A key part of their work entails integrating the programs of the different organizations it funds. Through collaboration, they hope to bring a multifaceted approach to tough social problems. They also tend to focus on specific neighborhoods. This is a relatively new venture that expects to grow its programs slowly and tackle only a few projects at a time.

As we approach the end of this philanthropic planning journey, we will suggest three areas of opportunity for corporate executives and business owners. These philanthropic opportunities not only cover important community needs, but offer you the ability to use your professional business skills to change the landscape of your communities. As you consider the arguments below, think about what made you successful in your own business and professional world:

- A vision
- Strong marketing skills
- Financial acumen
- Ability to foster collaborations
- Strong partnerships
- Willingness to take risks
- Willingness to admit mistakes and move on
- Ability to foster the right political connections

Each of these skills and others can be employed in the areas below:

Build Strong Neighborhoods

Socio-economic problems certainly need to be approached on an issue-by-issue basis to achieve the efficiencies afforded by economies of scale. However, many of our social ills result from dysfunctional families. Some argue that nothing really gets solved until we can find ways to build stable and effective families. There may be a middle ground here, and that involves a focus on neighborhoods. By building stronger neighborhoods, we encourage residents to improve the appearance of their homes and streets. This can lead to more parental involvement in schools, and subsequently, better schools, lower crime rates, and more constructive social and athletic opportunities for the youth. Then comes more commerce and with that more jobs. All of this leads to more and better housing and increased housing prices, which are good for investment.

This type of venture fits well with the skill set of business executives and entrepreneurs. You have the contacts and the skills to foster the collaboration needed. Many of you are knowledgeable about housing and real estate. You understand marketing and investments, all of which are needed. Engaging in this type of venture provides opportunities to build models that could have unlimited replication possibilities.

What, then, are ways you can contribute in an effort like this? First, you can provide some funds of your own and use your networks to gain collaborative funding. Your political connections or those of your company can be used to make sure the right city services get channeled to the neighborhood. In particular, you can ensure that all available governmental housing subsidies are taken advantage of – but not from the standpoint of having the government build homes like those they built in the past. Instead, strive to obtain incentives for residents to buy and maintain homes so that values increase. Go to the foundation community and other wealthy philanthropists to build day care centers or sports centers to house city youth athletic leagues. You can then use your entrepreneurial skills to do what *you* can do better than anyone else: create new businesses, by either bringing in businesses from outside the community or seeding new businesses for low-income residents, thus creating new jobs. After all, that's what all of this is about. Jobs lead to healthy neighborhoods and stable families.

Models for building strong, healthy neighborhoods are springing up. A prestigious Baltimore foundation, the Morris Goldseker Foundation of Maryland, initiated a wide-sweeping program to focus intense efforts on a couple of designated neighborhoods. They will hopefully be successful in establishing a model that can expand far beyond its initial sites.

Build Capacity in Non-profit Organizations

With few exceptions, funders over the years have stressed program development, measurable outcomes, and low operating overhead. Many people even believed that individuals working for non-profits do so out of love for the mission and do not care about money, as long as they are earning a supportable wage. Philanthropic strategies built around this way of thinking have failed and will continue to fail. The new venture philanthropy has begun to change this way of thinking. To begin with, more is being published on this topic, with a watershed study undertaken by the famed management consulting firm, McKinsey & Company. This study featured a detailed Capacity Assessment Grid that is useful in evaluating the management and structural capacity of a non-profit organization. It was funded by Venture Philanthropy Partners, whom we spoke about earlier.

This type of initiative is, again, well suited for the executive who has successfully built and managed powerful commercial enterprises. Non-profits have a range of needs; some require money, while others require expertise. Consider the following:

- Financial management, including cost accounting systems
- Strategic planning
- Board structure and governance
- Fund-raising organization
- Technology
- Legal counsel
- Human resource programs
- Program design
- Marketing
- Lobbying
- Program evaluation techniques
- CEO leadership training

Emerging initiatives are rapidly taking hold in communities around the country. An example is the work being done by the Eugene and Agnes E. Meyer Foundation in the Washington, D.C., area. They are particularly focusing on strengthening the organizational capacity of non-profits that serve low-income people and deal with neighborhood development.

Foster Entrepreneurs

A natural fit for the corporate executive, his or her company, and the business owner is to help others start their own business or secure a meaningful career. This endeavor does not necessarily require you to set up a new entity, as many communities have organizations dedicated to minority business development or job creation. What they may need is strong management oversight and people who can help them build collaborations that will facilitate their success.

Here is an interesting example of a venture designed to create jobs in the urban marketplace. There is a venture capital fund called Urban Growth Partners whose mission is to invest in urban enterprises that can generate job opportunities for low- and middle-income urban workers, as well as a decent financial return for its investors, which can include foundations.

They look for companies with a proven track record and capable management. They usually play a lead investing role and work with management to attract additional capital. Urban Growth Partners is based in Philadelphia and was initially underwritten by a group of foundations, insurance firms, and banks. The fund is administered by The Reinvestment Fund, which has a good record in finding companies that create jobs. The geographic focus is the Mid-Atlantic region. The story continues in Baltimore, where George Soros, through his Open Society Institute, issued a challenge to the philanthropic community to establish a $15 million fund for Baltimore. He offered to put up a considerable investment if other funders followed suit. They did, and a fund was established, to be managed through Urban Growth partners.

Room for Everyone

While venture philanthropy has done much to change the landscape of charitable giving, it does have its detractors. Critics are quick to point out that traditional venture capitalists have failures, as well as successes, and they spend too much time micro-managing organizations. They also charge that venture philanthropists focus on only a few projects at a time, effectively shutting the door on many smaller organizations that require community support. Also, they may be reluctant to cut off an organization whose model is not working, since they have dollars and their reputations already on the line. This is the concept of throwing good money after bad.

The venture philanthropist will fire back and say that ideas are worthless if they cannot be brought to market successfully. Only strong organizations can do that, so they need to invest in programs and in the organizations themselves. They also contend that foundations will pull the plug long before a program fulfills its mission because the foundations want to do something new.

The reality is that there is room for both the traditional foundation and the venture philanthropist. Intense focus on programs can be the domain of some foundations, while non-profit capacity building, neighborhood development, and entrepreneurialism can be left to the venture philanthropist.

ELEVEN

Your Advisory Team

If you embark on establishing a full-fledged charitable plan, you will not have to go it alone. A range of advisors dot the landscape to assist you with various phases of the journey. We will look at some of them:

Attorney

When setting up a charitable trust or a private foundation, your attorney is critical to the process as he or she is the only one qualified to draft the governing legal documents. Additionally, with foundations, there are filings that need to take place with the IRS and respective state authorities. Even if you set up a charitable gift annuity or a donor advised fund, you may want your attorney to review the documents.

You should be aware that the charitable field can be quite complex at times. Especially if you are engaging in some of the more advanced techniques, you should make sure your attorney is well versed on charitable tax matters. If not, find one of the many outstanding attorneys around the country who specialize in charitable activities. Attorneys who have expertise in this field are also well suited to advise you on the range of charitable alternatives, highlighting the advantages and disadvantages of each. More importantly, they should know what is most suitable for you and your family.

CPA

Your CPA is also in a good position to advise you on charitable structures. Additionally, CPAs can prepare all of the governmental tax filings at inception. Once your charitable structures are operating, your CPA then becomes involved with tax preparations.

Financial Institutions

Commercial and investment banking institutions can offer a suite of services related to your philanthropic structures. Some may be able to handle all facets except for the drafting of legal documents. For example, you may find some of these services available through your private banker or investment broker:

- Charitable tax planning
- Fiduciary administration of charitable trusts or foundations
- Investment management
- Investment consulting
- Tax preparation and providing tax schedules to your CPA
- Grant-making administration

Insurance Representatives

Where insurance is critical, you will naturally want to engage your insurance agent. It's likely you'll need your insurance agent when you plan a charitable remainder trust and want to attach a wealth replacement trust to it.

Planned Giving Officers

Most large charities and non-profit institutions have formal planned giving offices with experts there to assist you in structuring gifts. Keeping in mind that while they are motivated to direct you toward giving to their institution, their services and advice are free. Also, if you plan to give something to that particular institution anyway, you may as well talk to their people.

Fee-based Financial Planners

If you regularly use an independent financial planner who sells no products, you will certainly want to engage this person in the process, provided he or she is competent in the charitable field. This adviser should also be helpful in identifying which assets should go into the various structures, as he or she would be very familiar with your investment portfolio.

Philanthropic Advisers

A select group of advisers can assist you in developing grant-making strategies, including how to govern your foundation and the role your children and others should and can play. These experts also assist in setting up the process for reviewing and administering grant programs.

TWELVE

RESOURCES

When you engage in philanthropy today, you are very fortunate in that there is a rapidly emerging field of organizations designed to help you get started with and then to operate your philanthropic plan. An attractive feature of these organizations is that they provide different venues for meeting with other donors and philanthropists. In addition to these organizations, there is much written about the field of philanthropy. The challenge is to find the organizations and literature that fit your particular situation. This chapter features resources available to help you in this process. We will survey some of the publications, industry organizations, and grant-making associations. This list is, by no means, exhaustive. It is just intended to be a start, but is geared toward those resources that might at least be applicable to the executive and business owner.

Publications

The Tools & Techniques of Charitable Planning
Stephen R. Leimberg, *et al.*
The National Underwriting Company
P. O. Box 14367
Cincinnati, Ohio 45250-0367

> This is a complete guide to virtually all of the different charitable structures, including charitable trusts, gift annuities, pooled income funds, foundations, supporting organizations, donor advised funds, and other techniques. The material is presented in a way that it can serve the needs of the student, as well as the advanced practitioner, who can use this as a handy reference. Of particular value for the executive and business owner are sections indicating when each technique should be used, along with the advantages and disadvantages of each. Also included in

the text are charitable trust forms, various IRS forms and filing information, and a complete range of valuation tables.

Contemporary Estate Planning: A Definitive Guide to Planning and Practice
Roy M. Adams, Kirkland & Ellis
Cannon Financial Institute, Inc., Publication

This publication overall is a comprehensive guide to estate planning, including charitable giving. It especially covers charitable remainder and lead trusts and some advanced techniques, such as zeroed-out CLATs, the sale of CLT remainder interests to GST-exempt trusts, and charitable limited partnerships.

Invest in Charity: A Donor's Guide to Charitable Giving
Ron Jordan and Katelyn L. Quynn
John Wiley & Sons, Inc.
605 Third Avenue
New York, N.Y. 10158-0012

This publication covers some of the structural and tax aspects of various charitable giving strategies. In addition, it reviews many of the different assets you can transfer into charitable structures, including real estate, tangible personal property, intangible assets, life insurance, and business interests. The book goes beyond structure and discusses ways to develop your giving plans. Among the areas covered are structuring gifts, selecting charities, and working with professional advisers.

First Steps in Starting a Foundation
John A. Edie
Council on Foundations
1828 L Street, N. W.
Washington, D.C.

When you decide to set up a foundation, this is the how-to book. It covers the range of foundation options, including private family foundations, community foundations, operating foundations, supporting organizations, and others. There is a discussion of the various tax regulations surrounding private foundations, with sample tax forms, articles of incorporation, by-laws, and trust agreements. Specifically, the book describes the process for applying to the IRS for your tax-exempt status.

Don't Just Give It Away
Renata J. Rafferty
Chandler House Press
Worcester, Massachusetts

> Before embarking on a grant-making plan, you may wish to read a book like this. In an easy-to-read format, it provides thoughts on establishing philanthropic objectives, selecting spheres of influence, performing due diligence on and selecting charities, determining your type of gift, and measuring the performance of the charitable recipient.

Grantmaking Basics: A Field Guide for Funders
Barbara D. Kibbe, Fred Setterberg, and Colburn S. Wilbur
Council on Foundations
1828 L Street, N.W.
Washington, D.C. 20036

> Subsidized by the David and Lucile Packard Foundation, this book serves as both a guide and a type of workbook for conducting grant-making activities. Of particular impact are the segments on reviewing grant proposals, reviewing non-profit finances, and conducting site visits.

New Philanthropy Benchmarking: Wisdom for the Passionate
Kristina Anna Kazarian
United University Press

> This is something of a landmark book in the "new philanthropy" era. Its purpose is to show how capitalists can strive for the same success in the social sector as they achieved in the commercial sector. The author presents her message through "seven wisdom points" and features seven leading capitalists and philanthropists. She especially makes a case for transferring successful benchmarking techniques from the commercial to the social sector.

A Founder's Guide to the Family Foundation
Douglas K. Freeman and Lee Hausner
Council on Foundations
1828 L Street, N. W.
Washington, D.C. 20036

> This booklet is an easy-to-follow guide on the key elements of setting up a family foundation. Aside from covering the process for making grants, it devotes space to such aspects as governing

the foundation and the role of the family. In particular, it features the issue of providing a clear path for succession.

Starting a Private Foundation
New Ventures in Philanthropy
Forum of Regional Association of Grantmakers
1828 L Street, N. W.
Washington, D.C.

> Originally published by the Southeast Council of Foundations, this is a concise primer on organizing and operating a private family foundation. It provides insights on when one should select the foundation option and includes a summary of the major tax rules and issues.

A Plan of One's Own: A Woman's Guide to Philanthropy
The Baltimore Giving Project
New Ventures in Philanthropy
Association of Baltimore Area Grantmakers
2 East Read Street
Baltimore, Maryland 21202-2470

> A project under the New Ventures in Philanthropy initiative (see below), this is a very timely and thorough guide for women donors and philanthropists. It not only contains comprehensive educational information on the mechanics of charitable giving, but also includes a range of topics that is of special interest to women as philanthropists.

Family Foundations and the Law: What You Need to Know
John A. Edie
Council on Foundations
1828 L Street, N. W.
Washington, D.C. 20036

> This book covers the range of legal and tax issues you need to be aware of when operating a family foundation. Its topics include charitable deduction limitations, tax compliance rules, and international grant-making regulations.

Grants to Individuals by Private Foundations
Edward J. Beckwith and David Marshall (Baker & Hostetler)
Council on Foundations Publication
1828 L Street, N. W.

Washington, D.C. 20036

> This is an authoritative guide involving grants to individuals. The publication covers legal considerations and IRS tax rules as they relate to individual grant recipients. Also included are relevant IRS code sections and specific revenue rulings covering these activities.

A Guide to Strategic Planning for Corporate Contributions
Cynthia D. Giroud, revised by Lori A. Vacek
Council on Foundations
1828 L Street, N. W.
Washington, D.C. 20036

> This book presents a case for integrating philanthropic goals with your company's strategic mission and objectives, as well as a process for doing so.

Effective Capacity Building in Nonprofit Organizations
Prepared for Venture Philanthropy Partners
McKinsey & Company

> This study, prepared by perhaps the most widely recognized consulting firm in the world, addresses the issue of capacity building in a comprehensive way. The study first attempts to define capacity building. It then illustrates examples of successful capacity building initiatives. The capstone of the study is the presentation of a framework for assessing the capacity strength of an organization.

Inspired Philanthropy: Creating a Giving Plan
Tracy Gary and Melissa Kohner
Chardon Press
3781 Broadway
Oakland, California 94611

> This book is unique in its creative presentation. Through a series of exercises, the authors show you how to develop a vision, establish a plan, and implement a grants program. Throughout the book are short examples of what others have done.

The Insider's Guide to Philanthropy
Joel J. Orosz
Publication of the W. K. Kellogg Foundation
Jossey-Bass, a Wiley Company
San Francisco, California

Written by an insider to grant-making, this book can be an intensive guide for the program officer or anyone deeply connected to the grants process. It covers the full range of grants management, including the review of programs, site visits, responding to proposals, presenting funding documents to approving boards, and managing large projects.

High Impact Philanthropy
Kay Sprinkel Grace and Alan L. Wendroff
John Wiley & Sons
New York, N. Y.

This is written from the standpoint of the nonprofit organization seeking what are termed "transformational" grants. It is an insightful guide for organizations that are heading in new directions and wish to attract significant gifts to accomplish their aims. Alternatively, for the funder, it can be a useful guide in evaluating nonprofits and assessing the potential impact of a significant gift.

Industry Organizations

Council on Foundations
1828 L Street N.W.
Washington, D.C. 20036
www.cof.org

Established in 1949, the Council provides a range of services to family, community, and corporate foundations. For its contributing members, the Council can provide legal consultation, discounted publications, conferences, and technical grant-making assistance. Additionally, it serves as a key political advocacy arm for the foundation community.

The Philanthropic Initiative, Inc.
77 Franklin Street
Boston, Massachusetts 02110
www.tpi.org

Founded in 1989, the Philanthropic Initiative is a nonprofit consulting firm serving individual donors, family foundations, community foundations, and corporations. It generally assists these entities in designing a wide range of philanthropic programs. Additionally, TPI engages in furthering the entire field of philanthropy through its own research, publishing, and donor education initiatives.

The Philanthropy Roundtable
1150 17th Street N.W.
Washington, D.C.
www.philanthropyroundtable.org

This organization is a national association of over 600 individual donors, corporate giving officers, foundation staff and trustees, and professional advisers. It was founded in the late 1970s to provide a forum where independent grant-makers could readily access their peers. The organization features a full program of conferences and publications.

Association of Small Foundations
733 15th Street N.W.
Washington, D.C. 20005
www.smallfoundations.org

Established in 1995, this organization's purpose is to assist those foundations with small staffs. Its services span a wide range of topics and issues. For its members, it provides newsletters, director's and officer's liability insurance, field of interest guides, discounts on publications, trustee leadership seminars, and access to "foundation-in-a-box," which is a compilation of articles by more than 140 authors on all topics of foundation management.

Independent Sector
1200 Eighteenth Street, N.W.
Washington, D.C. 20036
www.indepsec.org

Founded in 1980, this entity is a coalition of more than 800 private and corporate foundations and other voluntary organizations. Its purpose is to provide a forum to promote volunteerism and charitable giving. It actively publishes articles to support its cause and to educate public leaders.

The Foundation Center
79 Fifth Avenue
New York, N.Y. 10003-3076
www.fdncenter.org

Founded in 1956 by a group of foundations, this organization was established to become an authoritative source of information on foundations, corporate giving, and philanthropy in general. It publishes a variety of materials, including *The Foundation*

Directory, an annual compilation of key facts on about 10,000 of the country's foundations. Users of the Center's publications and services include grant seekers, grant makers, researchers, policy makers, and the public.

The National Center for Family Philanthropy
1220 Nineteenth Street N.W.
Washington, D.C. 20036
www.ncfp.org

Established in 1997 by a group of private philanthropists, this organization is focused on the issues that are particular to family donors. It helps families integrate their personal values and circumstances with their charitable goals. Like other organizations, it publishes materials and arranges conferences.

Regional Associations of Grant Makers

A third resource available to grant makers is the overall network of grant-maker associations established around the country. Called "regional associations of grant makers," sometimes referred to as RAGs, these organizations are membership associations formed by private foundations, companies, and individual donors to further the cause of philanthropy in their cities, states, and regions. Each of the regional associations then works in close partnership with their national umbrella organization, the Forum of Regional Associations of Grantmakers. The national group is also currently overseeing an initiative called "New Ventures in Philanthropy," which supports new coalitions across the country with the aim of increasing charitable giving in both traditional and non-traditional ways. We will consider each of these three entities:

Regional Association of Grantmakers

These organizations are locally run and governed by their own board of directors. They generally provide their members (private foundations, individual donors, and companies) with educational programs across a range of topics important to funders. These topics can include issues related to healthcare, economic development, substance abuse, education, and neighborhood development. Additionally, there are educational sessions related to developing grant-making policies, investment management, and foundation governance. These regional associations also publish pamphlets and short books of interest to their constituencies. RAGs can provide services to individuals and companies interested in starting new philanthropic programs. For instance, they can explain the various structural options, assist in formulating a grants program, or just provide prospective donors with sample documents and policy statements.

Forum of Regional Associations of Grantmakers

This is the national network of local RAGs. It encompasses 28 regional associations that collectively include more than 4,000 foundations and grant-makers. It provides members with a range of benefits. A key benefit is the ability to network with your counterparts from across the country. The Forum holds an annual meeting for staff and board leadership from the regional associations. It holds a CEO Summer Seminar, which is a leadership development program for member CEOs. Additionally, it holds regular conference calls and topic-specific and audience-specific national meetings. For the RAGs and their members, the Forum provides educational materials related to legislative issues and philanthropy in general. Discounts are generally available to members on products from other organizations, such as the Council on Foundations.

New Ventures in Philanthropy

Born in 1998 through a collaboration of national funders, including the Ford and Kellogg Foundations, New Ventures in Philanthropy inaugurated a bold new step in the charitable field. The funders wanted to launch an initiative that would foster innovative approaches to creating new foundations and corporate giving programs. The project got under way with a $10 million initial grant. The funders approached The Philanthropic Initiative to lay out the program, which resembles a series of "laboratory experiments." The objective is to develop models that can then be adopted by others. Local grant-making organizations and coalitions were invited to submit proposals for funding, and today there are about 40 initiatives under way. The program itself is managed by the Forum of Regional Association of Grantmakers. To locate a program near you, call the Forum at 202-467-0383, or visit their Web site at www.rag.org/promote/grantees.html.

THIRTEEN

LEADERSHIP

More than any other class of person, you, the corporate executive and business owner, have the skill sets to radically transform the philanthropic world. Moreover, you can change the way we fund and operate some of our country's non-profit social and human service entities. You can employ the same creative, operational, and sales skills you used so successfully in building your own businesses to build the infrastructure of neighborhoods and the non-profit organizations themselves.

Executives take the heat when their companies falter, when some of their colleagues misbehave, and when their boards provide them with lucrative compensation packages. On the other hand, very few seem to criticize Bill Gates, whose foundation is in the billions of dollars. Philanthropy is good business. It is good for your company and for your own personal prestige.

Finally, despite our country's great riches, we seem to continuously suffer from the social ravages of hunger, homelessness, and crime. Consequently, these problems will require more innovative leadership. Certainly this leadership lies in creating new models, but equally so, it lies in making sure those organizations executing the models have the resources and skills to do so successfully. This is the time for you to stand up and lead, transferring your skills at creating shareholder value into creating community wealth.

BIBLIOGRAPHY

Pamphlets

"Building to Last: A Grantmaker's Guide to Strengthening Nonprofit Organizations." Philadelphia: The Conservation Company, 2001.

"Effective Capacity Building in Nonprofit Organizations." Reston: Venture Philanthropy Partners, 2001.

"Family Foundations Now – And Forever?" Washington, D.C.: Council on Foundations, 1991.

"Great Neighborhoods, Great Cities." Baltimore: Morris Goldseker Foundation, 2001.

"Philanthropy for the Wise Donor-Investor." Boston: The Philanthropic Initiative, Inc, 2001.

"Sounding the Call for Philanthropy: The Promotion Issue." Boston: The Philanthropic Initiative, Inc, 2001.

"So You Want To Give?" Washington, D.C.: Forum of Regional Associations of Grantmakers, 1999.

"Starting A Private Foundation." Washington, D.C.: Forum of Regional Associations of Grantmakers, 1999.

"The Maryland Business Giving Workbook." Baltimore: Association of Baltimore Area Grantmakers and The Baltimore Giving project, 2002.

"When and How to Use External Evaluators." Baltimore: The Association of Baltimore Area Grantmakers, 2002.

Books

Adams, Roy M. *Contemporary Estate Planning.* New York: Cannon Financial Institute, 2000.

Edie, John A. *First Steps in Starting A Foundation.* 5th ed. Washington, D.C.: Council on Foundations, 2001.

Gary, Tracy, and Melissa Kohner. *Inspired Philanthropy.* Berkeley: Chardon Press, 1998.

Grace, Kay S., and Alan L. Wendroff. *High Impact Philanthropy.* New York: John Wiley and Sons, 2001.

Grogan, Paul S., and Tony Proscio. *Comeback Cities*. Boulder: Westview Press, 2000.

Jordon, Ron, and Katelyn L. Quynn. *Invest In Charity*. New York: John Wiley and Sons, 2001.

Kazarian, Kristina A. *New Philanthropy Benchmarking*. Providence: United UP, 2002.

Kibbe, Barbara D., Fred Setterberg, and Colburn S. Wilbur. *Grantmaking Basics*. Washington, D.C.: Council on Foundations, 1999.

Leimberg, Stephan R. *The Tools and Techniques of Charitable Planning*. Cincinnati: The National Underwriter Company, 2001.

Leimberg, Stephan R. *The Tools and Techniques of Estate Planning*. 12th ed. Cincinnati: The National Underwriter Company, 2001.

Orosz, Joel J. *The Insider's Guide to Grantmaking*. San Francisco: Jossey-Bass, 2000.

Rafferty, Reneta J. *Don't Just Give It Away*. Rochester: Chandler House Press, 1999.

Wagner, William J. *The Trust Handbook*. Cincinnati: National Underwriter, 1997.

Magazine Articles

Adams, Roy M. "A Smart Idea For Giving To Charities – And Family." *Financial Advisor* (January 2003): n. pag. 79-80

Byrne, John A. "The New Face of Philanthropy." *BusinessWeek*. (December 2, 2002): n. pag. 82-94

Bostwick, Jarrett. "Choose Supporting Organizations." *Trusts And Estates* (January 2003): n. pag. 25-31

Farber, Jason H., and David W. Newman. "A Guide to Donor Advised Funds." *Trusts And Estates* (November 2000): n. pag. 70-80

Grimm, Robert T. "From 'Retail' to 'Wholesale' Giving." *Foundation News and Commentary* (July 2002): n. pag. 26

Hoyt, Christopher R. "Solutions For Estates Overloaded with Retirement Plan Accounts: The Credit Shelter CRUT." *Trusts And Estates* (May 2002): n. pag. 21-29

Kosminsky, Jay. "Venture Philanthropy – A New Model for Corporate Giving." *Fund Raising Management* (August 1997): n. pag. 28-32

Kramer, Mark R., and Michael E. Porter. "Philanthropy's New Agenda: *Creating Value.*" *Harvard Business Review* (November 1999): n. pag 121 -130.

Krebsbach, Karen. "The New Face of Philanthropy." *Bank Investment Marketing* (February 2002): n. pag. 26-31

Lintott, James A., and Roger D. Silk. "Building Solid Foundations." *Trusts And Estates* (August 2002): n. pag. 41-47

McCarthy, Stephen J. "Family Foundations – Insights On Best Practices." *Trusts And Estates* (October 2000): n. pag. 14-16

Miree, Kathryn W. "Wanted: Overseers." *Trusts And Estates* (October 2002): n. pag. 52-58

Sellers, Patricia. "The New Breed." *Fortune* (November 18, 2002): n. pag. 66-76

Smith, Craig. "The New Corporate Philanthropy." *Harvard Business Review* (May 1994): n. pag. 105-116

Teitell, Conrad. "2002 Tax Primer." *Trusts And Estates* (June 2002): n. pag. CG11-CG20

Useem, Jerry. "From Heroes to Goats ... And Back Again?" *Fortune* (November 18, 2002): n. pag. 41-48

Useem, Jerry. "Tyrants, Statesmen, and Destroyers (A Brief History of the CEO)." *Fortune* (November 1, 2002): n. pag. 41-48

Vasella, Daniel. "Confessions of a CEO." *Fortune* (November 18, 2002): n. pag. 109-116

Worthington, Dr. Daniel G. "Revised Charitable Trust Rules: Rethinking Short-term Trusts." *Trusts And Estates* (March 2000): n. pag. 20-24

ABOUT THE AUTHOR

Howard Weiss is a Senior Vice President and Wealth Management Consultant at Bank of America, specializing in the family office and private foundation markets. He advises clients on how to establish and run family offices and also provides strategic advice to wealthy families in the areas of investment policy, concentrated equity strategies, fiduciary structures, risk management, wealth transfer and philanthropic management. In the area of private foundations, he assists clients with governance, investment policies and grantmaking.

Weiss holds a number of positions within the Baltimore / Washington foundation communities. He is a member of the investment committee of the Morris Goldseker Foundation of Maryland and is a director of the Mary and Daniel Loughran Foundation. Additionally, Weiss is Treasurer and a member of the board of directors of the Association of Baltimore Area Grantmakers.

Weiss has also been active in the Baltimore non-profit community. He just completed a three-year term as Chairman of the Board of LifeBridge Health, a multi-hospital health care system. He has also served on the boards of the National Aquarium in Baltimore, the Center for Poverty Solutions, the B&O Railroad Museum, the American Jewish Committee, the Lyric Foundation and the Northwest Hospital Center.

Weiss has been with Bank of America and its predecessors for 18 years. Joining Maryland National Bank's Trust Division in 1985, Weiss served as its Chief Investment Officer and later as the Head of Personal Asset Management and Fiduciary Services. When NationsBank purchased Maryland National in 1993, Weiss became head of Personal Trust and later Private Banking for the greater Baltimore market. In that position, he led an integrated trust, investment management and credit business. He also spearheaded an effort to establish a private banking office for Bank of America in Philadelphia as well as a Delaware Trust Company in Wilmington.

Prior to joining Bank of America, Weiss was with Equibank in Pittsburgh, where he served as the Chief Investment Officer and Manager of the Trust Division over a five year period. He also served in the international Banking Division for six years, working in a variety of positions including Head of International Operations, Director of Correspondent Banking and Comptroller & Operations Manager of the Luxembourg Branch.

Executive Reports

Targeted Reports Featuring Hundreds of C-Level Perspectives

Executive Reports: How to Get an Edge in Business

This insider look at getting an edge in business is written by C-Level executives (CEOs, CFOs, CTOs, CMOs) from over 300 Fortune 100 companies. Each executive shares their knowledge on how to get an edge in business, from getting smart on new companies/industries quickly to creating additional value for clients to increasing your breadth of knowledge in your area of expertise. Also covered are over 250 specific, proven innovative strategies and methodologies practiced by leading executives of the world that have helped them gain an edge. This report is designed to give you insight into the leading executives of the world, and assist you in developing additional "special skills" that can help you be an even more successful professional. $279 – 70 Pages, 8.5 x 11

Executive Reports: The Industry Guide for Client Acquisition & Retention

This insider look at over 30 major industries and professions is the ideal tool for professionals who need to "get smart fast" before a client meeting, sales pitch or other event. Each industry overview has sections written by current, leading C-Level executives (CEOs, CFOs, CTOs, CMOs, Partners) from their respective industries and enables you to speak intelligently with anyone after being "briefed" by a leading executive from that industry The report is now a "how to sell report," but rather a report that enables you to understand an industry's/company's pain in order to better sell your products/services. Over 200 executives from Global 1000 companies such as GE, Amex, Coke, AT&T, Duke Energy and companies from every other major industry have contributed to this brief. This report also includes a special section on ethics and dealing with clients/prospective clients according to new industry standard ethical guidelines. $549 – 560 Pages, 8.5 x 11

BEST SELLING BOOKS

Reference

Business Travel Bible – Must Have Phone Numbers, Business Resources & Maps
The Golf Course Locator for Business Professionals – Golf Courses Closest to Largest Companies, Law Firms, Cities & Airports
Business Grammar, Style & Usage – Rules for Articulate and Polished Business Writing and Speaking
ExecRecs – Executive Recommendations For The Best Business Products & Services
Executive Zen – Mental & Physical Health & Happiness for Busy Business Professionals
The C-Level Test – Business IQ & Personality Test for Professionals of All Levels
The Business Translator-Business Words, Phrases & Customs in Over 65 Languages
Small Business Bible – Phone Numbers, Business Resources, Financial, Tax & Legal Info
The Small Business Checkup – A Planning & Brainstorming Workbook for Your Business

Management

Corporate Ethics – The Business Code of Conduct for Ethical Employees
The Governance Game – Restoring Boardroom Excellence & Credibility in America
Inside the Minds: Leading CEOs – CEOs Reveal the Secrets to Leadership & Profiting in Any Economy
Inside the Minds: The Entrepreneurial Problem Solver – Entrepreneurial Strategies for Identifying Opportunities in the Marketplace
Inside the Minds: Leading Consultants – Industry Leaders Share Their Knowledge on the Art of Consulting
Inside the Minds: Leading Women – What It Takes to Succeed & Have It All in the 21st Century
Being There Without Going There: Managing Teams Across Time Zones, Locations and Corporate Boundaries

Technology

Inside the Minds: Leading CTOs – The Secrets to the Art, Science & Future of Technology
Software Product Management – Managing Software Development from Idea to Development to Marketing to Sales
Inside the Minds: The Telecommunications Industry – Leading CEOs Share Their Knowledge on The Future of the Telecommunications Industry
Web 2.0 AC (After Crash) – The Resurgence of the Internet and Technology Economy
Inside the Minds: The Semiconductor Industry – Leading CEOs Share Their Knowledge on the Future of Semiconductors

Venture Capital/Entrepreneurial

Term Sheets & Valuations – A Detailed Look at the Intricacies of Term Sheets & Valuations
Deal Terms – The Finer Points of Deal Structures, Valuations, Term Sheets, Stock Options and Getting Deals Done
Inside the Minds: The Ways of the VC – Identifying Opportunities, Assessing Business Models and What it Takes to Land an Investment From a VC

Inside the Minds: Leading Deal Makers – Leveraging Your Position and the Art of Deal Making

Inside the Minds: Entrepreneurial Momentum – Gaining Traction for Businesses of All Sizes to Take the Step to the Next Level

Inside the Minds: The Entrepreneurial Problem Solver – Entrepreneurial Strategies for Identifying Opportunities in the Marketplace

Inside the Minds: JumpStart – Launching Your Business Venture, Profitably and Successfully

Legal

Inside the Minds: Privacy Matters – Leading Privacy Visionaries Share Their Knowledge on How Privacy on the Internet Will Affect Everyone

Inside the Minds: Leading Lawyers – Leading Managing Partners Reveal the Secrets to Professional and Personal Success as a Lawyer

Inside the Minds: The Innovative Lawyer – Leading Lawyers Share Their Knowledge on Using Innovation to Gain an Edge

Inside the Minds: Leading Labor Lawyers – Labor Chairs Reveal the Secrets to the Art & Science of Labor Law

Inside the Minds: Leading Litigators – Litigation Chairs Revel the Secrets to the Art & Science of Litigation

Inside the Minds: Leading IP Lawyers – IP Chairs Reveal the Secrets to the Art & Science of IP Law

Inside the Minds: Leading Deal Makers – The Art of Negotiations & Deal Making

Inside the Minds: The Corporate Lawyer – Corporate Chairs on the Successful Practice of Business Law

Financial

Inside the Minds: Leading Accountants – The Golden Rules of Accounting & the Future of the Accounting Industry and Profession

Inside the Minds: Leading Investment Bankers – Leading I-Bankers Reveal the Secrets to the Art & Science of Investment Banking

Inside the Minds: The Financial Services Industry – The Future of the Financial Services Industry & Professions

Building a $1,000,000 Nest Egg – 10 Strategies to Gaining Wealth at Any Age

Inside the Minds: The Return of Bullish Investing

Inside the Minds: The Invincibility Shield for Investors

Marketing/Advertising/PR

Inside the Minds: Leading Marketers–Leading Chief Marketing Officers Reveal the Secrets to Building a Billion Dollar Brand

Inside the Minds: Leading Advertisers – Advertising CEOs Reveal the Tricks of the Advertising Profession

Inside the Minds: The Art of PR – Leading PR CEOs Reveal the Secrets to the Public Relations Profession

Inside the Minds: PR Visionaries – PR CEOS Reveal the Golden Rules to Becoming a Senior Partner With Your Clients

Inside the Minds: The Art of Building a Brand – Leading Advertising & PR CEOs Reveal the Secrets Behind Successful Branding Strategies

The Best of Guerrilla Marketing – Marketing on a Shoestring Budget

To Order or For Customized Suggestions From an Aspatore Business Editor, Please Call 1-866-Aspatore (277-2867) Or Visit www.Aspatore.com